How to become more creative

How to become more creative

101 REWARDING WAYS
TO DEVELOP
YOUR POTENTIAL TALENT

by ALEX F. OSBORN, L. H. D.
AUTHOR OF *APPLIED IMAGINATION*

New York
CHARLES SCRIBNER'S SONS

COPYRIGHT SOURCES QUOTED

Adler, Mortimer, *How to Read a Book*, Simon and Schuster, New York, 1940.

Alger, Joseph, *Get in There and Paint*, T. Y. Crowell, New York, 1946.

Barton, Bruce, *The Man Nobody Knows*, The Bobbs-Merrill Company, New York, 1925.

Bauer, Dr. William Waldo, *Stop Annoying Your Children*, The Bobbs-Merrill Company, New York, 1947.

Broadley, Charles V. and Margaret E., *Know Your Real Abilities*, Whittlesey House, McGraw-Hill Book Co., 1948.

Burroughs, John, *The Heart of Burroughs' Journals*, edited by Clara Barrus, Houghton Mifflin Co., Boston, 1928.

Churchill, Winston S., "Painting as a Pastime" from *Amid These Storms*, Charles Scribner's Sons, New York, 1932.

Conant, James B., *On Understanding Science*, Yale University Press, New Haven, 1947.

Crawford, Robert P., *Think for Yourself*, McGraw-Hill Book Co., Inc., New York, 1937.

Dimnet, Ernest, *The Art of Thinking*, Simon and Schuster, New York, 1929.

Dunn, David, *Try Giving Yourself Away*, Updegraff Press, Scarsdale, 1947.

Hepner, Harry W., *Psychology Applied to Life and Work*, Prentice-Hall, Inc., New York, 1941.

Hunt, Peter, *Peter Hunt's Workbook*, Prentice-Hall, Inc., New York, 1945.

Kephart, Horace, *Camping and Woodcraft*, The Macmillan Company, New York, 1947.

Liebman, Joshua Loth, *Peace of Mind*, Simon and Schuster, New York, 1946.

Link, Henry C., *The Way to Security*, Doubleday and Co., Inc., New York, 1951.

Magoun, F. Alexander, *Love and Marriage*, Harper and Bros., New York, 1948.

Maugham, W. Somerset, *A Writer's Notebook*, Doubleday and Co., Inc., New York, 1949.

Mearns, Hughes, *Creative Power*, Doubleday Doran, New York, 1929.

Mearns, Hughes, *The Creative Adult*, Doubleday Doran, New York, 1940.

Mencken, Henry Louis, *The American Language*, Alfred A. Knopf, New York, 1945.

O'Connor, Johnson, *Ideaphoria*, Human Engineering Laboratory, Boston, 1945.

Overstreet, Harry Allen, *The Mature Mind*, W. W. Norton & Co., New York, 1949.

Overstreet, Harry Allen, *Let Me Think*, The Macmillan Company, New York, 1940.

Paine, Albert Bigelow, *Mark Twain*, Harper & Bros., New York, 1912.

Peale, Norman Vincent, *A Guide to Confident Living*, Prentice-Hall, Inc., New York, 1948.

Peale, Norman Vincent, *You Can Win*, Abingdon-Cokesbury, New York, 1938.

Reik, Theodor, *Listening with the Third Ear*, Farrar, Straus & Co., New York, 1949.

Taylor, Robert Lewis, *The Running Pianist*, Doubleday and Co., Inc., New York, 1950.

Terzian, Lawrence, *How to Get the Job You Want*, Grosset and Dunlap, New York, 1950.

Wallas, Graham, *The Art of Thought*, Harcourt, Brace & Co., New York, 1926.

Webster, Polly, *How to Make Money at Home*, Whittlesey House, McGraw-Hill Book Co., Inc., New York, 1949.

Whitehead, Alfred North, *The Aims of Education*, The Macmillan Company, New York, 1929.

Woolf, James D. and Charles B. Roth, *How to Use Your Imagination to Make Money*, Whittlesey House, McGraw-Hill Book Co., Inc., New York, 1948.

DEDICATION

SOME CHURCHGOERS can't help but keep a running score on the mentality of their ministers. Thus, for thirty years, I watched my pastor's creative power grow from strength to strength. He built up his mind by *exercising* it in creative ways—exercising it more steadily, more strenuously, than any other man I know.

He provided living proof that the greater our creative *activity*, the greater our creative *ability*. For that reason, I honor this book by dedicating it to my friend,

DR. ALBERT GEORGE BUTZER

WHAT THIS BOOK SEEKS TO DO

BY THE AUTHOR

We do not claim that this book could transform wheelwrights into playwrights, chauffeurs into authors, or waiters into inventors. We aim only to enable our readers to become more creative than they otherwise might be — and thus achieve greater happiness for themselves and for others.

Up until quite recently, most educators maintained that nothing could be done to help people become more creative. Scientific research has since proved that creative potential can be measurably developed through schooling and practice.

Although thousands of educational institutions now teach the principles and procedures of creative problem-solving, relatively few people have as yet enjoyed the benefit of such schooling. Nearly all must therefore depend on their own day-to-day efforts to enhance their imaginative power.

Improvement in creative ability basically depends on a person's attitude. Therefore, we hope to help the reader acquire:

(1) A keener *realization* of the fact that each of us *is* blessed with creative potential.

(2) A stronger *desire* to become more creative.

(3) A better *understanding* of the creative principles and procedures which research has proved to be conducive to improvement of creative ability.

After indicating the leisure-time activities which can help develop creativeness, we discuss daily duties at work and at home. We will show that every problem, personal or otherwise, is a creative challenge. We will explain how to find better solutions to these problems by attacking them imaginatively. Thus we hope to help our readers build up their creative power—all the way through life—even during the sunset years.

ALEX F. OSBORN

1964

ABOUT THE AUTHOR

- Started career as reporter and part-time teacher.

- Salesman, then sales manager for factory.

- Co-founder of Batten, Barton, Durstine and Osborn.

- Trustee of Western Savings Bank. Director of Marine Trust Company.

- Former Vice-President of Community Chests and Councils of America. Recipient of National Red Feather Award for "distinguished social service."

- Trustee of Hamilton College from which he received Ph.B., Ph.M. and L.H.D. degrees.

- Former Vice-Chairman of governing body of University of Buffalo. Recipient of Chancellor's Medal for "dignifying Buffalo in the eyes of the world."

- Founder of Creative Education Foundation, a non-profit institution devoted to helping education do more to develop creative ability.

- Author of four books on creativity, including the most widely adopted textbook, *Applied Imagination* (now in its 14th printing).

CONTENTS

How to become more creative

Chapter 1

OUR GREATEST GIFT —

why do we so neglect it?

"NEARLY ALL OF US are imaginative in our childhood," said Walt Disney. "But, as we grow older, we tend to lose our power of imagination. Failure to flex our imaginative muscles is as deplorable as breaking down our physical strength through lack of proper exercise."

It is an accepted fact that nature endows nearly all of us at birth with plenty of creative potential. It is an obvious fact that, as our years roll on, some of us grow creatively richer, while others grow creatively poorer. This is mainly because we *lose* what we don't *use*—we build up that which we exercise.

Loss of imagination can be even *more* deplorable than loss of musculation. We can get along with less brawn in our later years. But to surmount the obstacles which age piles on our paths we need more than seasoned judgment—we need a well-trained imagination, kept in the pink by creative exercise all the way through life.

Professor Hughes Mearns devoted his entire career to the teaching of creativity. From 1926 to 1946 he headed the Department of Creative Education at New York University. Here's his summary:

"Creativity is like another heart. No one has found the source of its power, but no one doubts that the source is within us. It will keep us alive if we give it a chance to beat for us. If we let it be stilled, there is then no more life. It needs continual exercise. If we keep it going strong, it can help us more and more to meet the needs of living."

Unfortunately, Professor Mearns blazed a one-man trail which other educators have shunned. Even psychologists have all but ignored creativity. The newly elected president of the American Psychological Association recently stated: "The neglect of this subject is *appalling*."

The italics are mine; but the words are those of Dr. J. P. Guilford, head of psychology at the University of Southern California.

2.

When we say, "Joe knows his own mind," we merely mean that he is fairly definite. If any of us *fully* knew his own mind, he would know more than is known. Although scalpels are cutting through much of our ignorance about our gray matter, the world is still in the dark as to what sparks our thinking processes.

Electronic brains built out of metal and plastics can now do almost everything human minds can do. To some extent they can even perform feats of judgment. But, according to Dr. Howard H. Aiken, head of Harvard's Computation Laboratory, these mechanized minds can *never* achieve that highest type of human thinking—creative imagination.

By and large, our mental powers are fourfold:

1. *Absorptive power*—the ability to observe, and to apply attention.

2. *Retentive power*—the ability to memorize and to recall.

3. *Reasoning power*—the ability to analyze and to judge.

4. *Creative power*—the ability to visualize, to foresee, and to generate ideas.

In absorbing and retaining, we make our mind serve as a sponge. In logical reasoning and in creative imagining, we make our mind *think*.

The thinking mind finds it easier to judge than to create. Nearly all of our education tends to develop our critical faculty. And our experience likewise builds up our judgment.

"Shall I get up or turn over?" By deciding such questions from morn to night we continually flex our judicial muscles. And oddly enough, the more we exercise our judgment, the less likely we are to exercise our imagination. By overuse of our judicial power we may even tend to cramp our creative power.

3.

As a term, imagination covers a field so wide and so hazy that a leading educator has called it "an area which psychologists fear to tread." For imagination takes many forms —some of them wild, some of them futile, some of them creative.

The berserk varieties include hallucinations, obsessions and other abnormalities which are beyond the scope of this book.

The futile forms are fairly normal. They include such meanderings as sleep-dreams and day-dreams, and some harmful phases such as complexes, worry, and the blues. In these latter forms our emotions tend to make imagination work against us. However, to a worth-while degree, we can conquer such imaginings by means of creative thinking of the kinds set forth in later chapters.

The *photographic* forms of imagination give us our power of *visual imagery* by which our mind's eye can see even those things which we have never seen.

Through *speculative* imagination we can even picture a nonexistent mountain in Florida—and can even cap it with snow!

Through *reproductive* imagination we can bring back many a scene from the distant past. *Look!* I can now focus my imagination on my boyhood and see a little girl peering at me over our back-yard fence. *Listen!* I can even hear the words she actually said to me on that faraway day: "If you'll give me a bite of that apple, I'll give you a kiss." Thus imagination can add *audio* as well as *video* to memory.

The third photographic form is *structural visualization.* My friend Larry Bell of Bell Aircraft could look at a flat blueprint and see a new type of jet fighter streaking through the sky. My daughter Kay can scan a dress pattern and see herself standing before her mirror in a brand-new costume of her own making.

Now we come to the *vicarious, anticipative,* and *creative* forms of imagination. Although the first two of these types are not strictly creative, they can be used creatively.

Vicarious imagination serves as a bridge—enables us to be someone else. When a soap-opera listener pictures herself as the glamorous girl friend of her radio Valentino, she thus uses vicarious imagination—but *not* creatively. However, by putting herself in the shoes of a sick neighbor and thinking up how to help her, she can make a creative use of vicarious imagination.

When we let *anticipative* imagination poison our minds with dire pictures of what *may* happen, we are far from being creative. But when we make ourselves foresee the best, while preparing for the worst, we make a creative use of anticipative imagination.

The highest form of imagination is the truly *creative.* Through this we seek new slants on old facts. We reach beyond the facts at hand in search of facts not yet known. Thus, in this phase of creativity, we use imagination as a searchlight. We beam it hither and thither, into the known and the unknown. Thus we *"discover."*

Then, too, creative imagination can serve us as a mixer. Thus we use it to combine known elements in order to produce the unknown. By changing combinations, we turn out still more ideas—ideas which otherwise would not come to us. Thus we *"invent"*—whether it be a new plot, a new mousetrap, or a better way of living our lives.

4.

In an early edition of Webster's Dictionary, imagination was defined in part as "the *will* working on materials of memory." And there can be no question but that *effort* has a lot to do with creativity. The main reason our imaginations tend to backslide is that we coddle our brains, instead of beating them in search of ideas.

From a strictly physical standpoint, we have far more gray matter than we could ever use, even if we worked our minds to capacity. It is literally true that most of our brain centers (such as those which enable us to speak and to read) are in duplicate. The stand-by twin remains idle until its opposite number is injured or diseased. The spare can then be trained to take over.

Louis Pasteur had a stroke which destroyed half his brain; yet he made some of his greatest discoveries after that. A New Yorker underwent an operation in which the front left third of his brain was removed. Later he took a test which showed an extraordinarily high I.Q. Tʰ are are countless such cases.

But we who have all our brains—do we ever really think up to our capacities? Surely, we admit that Professor William James of Harvard was right in saying: "Compared to what we ought to be, we are only half awake. We are making use of only a small part of our mental resources."

George Bernard Shaw agreed with James but, as usual, dramatized his statement: "Few people think more than two or three times a year. I have made an international reputation by thinking once or twice a week."

Such thinking mainly refers to judicial thinking—analyzing, comparing, concluding. When it comes to *creative* thinking—conscious effort to think up wanted ideas—even Shaw could not exaggerate our failure to make full use of our brains.

James D. Woolf was long a star in one of the toughest of "idea professions"—advertising. Out of those 30 years of his came this conclusion: "My experience convinces me that imagination is not a gift; it is an habitual way of *using* your mind. Many times people have said to me, 'I can't think up ideas—I guess I was born without imagination.' My answer to such confused individuals is always the same: 'How hard do you try? Have you really made a determined effort over a long period of time to train yourself to think creatively?'"

Too many of us look upon imagination as something that will run itself—like a stomach or other organ which works automatically under the effortless guidance of the sympathetic nervous system. Accordingly, we let our imagination push us around. Unless we do something about pushing it around, it will not only shortchange us, but will grow less and less usable.

5.

All agree that imagination is the pristine power of the human mind—the divine spark which makes man "the paragon of animals," as Shakespeare put it.

Civilization is the product of creative thinking. As Henry J. Taylor has said, "Imagination lit every lamp in this country, produced every article we use, built every church, made every discovery, performed every act of kindness and progress, created more and better things for more people. It is the priceless ingredient for a better day."

A Yale professor has estimated that—thanks to the machines which have been created by man—the average person now has available to him a work power equal to the muscle power of 120 slaves.

That such progress can continue, Charles F. Kettering, for one, felt certain: "Every time you tear a leaf off a calendar you present a new place for new ideas and progress. All along the future years is spaced new information. It comes by inventions, by discoveries, and by research. We can't stop this development because we know practically nothing about anything. We have it all in front of us."

When it comes to business, ideas are almost everything. Their value can often exceed that of any asset on any financial statement.

Dr. S. L. Wells reported to the American Association of Applied and Professional Psychologists the results of his study of a high-salaried group of people in comparison with a group of average salary. In four intelligence tests, these two groups rated about equal in all respects except one—creativity. Those who had climbed higher were the ones who could think up more things to do and more ways of doing them. As Montaigne wrote: "A strong imagination begetteth opportunity."

And when it comes to our personal affairs, nothing can brighten our lives as much as a well-trained and well-directed imagination. The very use of it can be an abiding joy. Creative effort, said Eliel Saarinen, is the "inner drive for inner satisfaction."

6.

Since time began, the masters of thought have paid tribute to the creative power of man's mind. And yet, modern psychology had thrown but little new light on the subject prior to 1950. Educators had tended to treat creativity as if it were a skeleton in the closet.

In charging education with ignoring creativity, Dr. J. P. Guilford pointed out: "The evidences of neglect are so obvious that I need not give proof. But the extent of the neglect I had not realized until recently. To obtain a more tangible idea of the situation, I examined the index of the *Psychological Abstracts* for each year since its origin. Of approximately 121,000 titles listed in the past 23 years, only 186 were indexed as definitely bearing on the subject of creativity. The topics under which such references are listed include creativity, imagination, originality, thinking, and tests in these areas. In other words, less than two-tenths of one per cent of the books and articles indexed in the *Abstracts* for approximately the past quarter century bear directly on this subject." So spoke Dr. Guilford in 1950.

In my favorite text on Applied Psychology, an 800-page tome by Dr. George W. Crane, the index listed over 1,000 references. Twenty of these concern advertising. Eleven concern sex. One each refers to fingernails, funerals, Clark Gable, horseback riding, idiots, obesity, opium, pipe smoking, sour grapes, and stuttering. But in that whole index of this great text on applied psychology, there was no mention whatsoever of creativity, or ideas, or imagination!

Even encyclopedias seemed to pretend that there was no such thing as imagination. My favorite reference work is *The Columbia Encyclopedia*. When I asked its editor why this great tome omitted all reference to creativity, he explained that his staff had made several stabs at writing suitable pieces, but had failed to produce anything "informative enough."

This "appalling neglect" could not have been due to any doubt as to the existence of imagination or as to its importance. The explanation is that scientific research had not as yet thrown enough light on the subject.

7.

It may matter but little to some of us that imagination is the light that lit the world—or that ideas can be the stepping-stones to our success in business or in a profession. But it must matter to all of us that, through active use of imagination, every one of us can get more out of life.

Even from the standpoint of personality, creativity can do far more than cosmetics, or clothes, or manners. H. A. Overstreet made this observation: "People who are creatively alert are much more interesting than those who are not. They seem almost to belong to a different species, or perhaps to a higher level of evolution. They see not only what is but what might be; and the power to see what might be is one of the chief traits that distinguish human beings from one another."

As for getting along with oneself, our contentment largely depends on whether we are creative or non-creative. Especially in our earlier years, all of us possess a creative urge. When this yen has too little outlet, frustration sets in; and such frustration undermines happiness.

According to the findings of the Human Engineering Laboratory, much of our restlessness arises from disuse of our aptitudes. Our talents are constantly craving outlet; more than that, they are constantly craving development. When we dam them up, they torment us. Thus the cause of our discontent can often be traced to failure to exercise our creative aptitudes. To paraphrase Ben Franklin: "To cease to think creatively is but little different from ceasing to live."

Our global chaos can't help but mar the happiness of every thinking person. To overcome gloom and worry, we have to fight harder than ever. Religious faith can help keep us at our best in this battle. But the right use of imagination can help a lot, too—a fact which later chapters will spell out.

Professor D. K. Winebrenner summarized this philosophy in these words: "We are all partly dead, for we do not use all of our powers. He who creates most is he who lives the most abundant life. The creative individual can be free in a prison cell; but the unimaginative soul is a walking zombie in a great unknown."

Yes, the one overshadowing reason why we should keep ourselves creatively alert is that in this way we can make our lives more worthwhile to ourselves as well as to others. The fact is that the lamp which lit the world can light our lives.

Chapter 2

ALL OF US are born

with creative talent

ALL OF US are blessed with some degree of imagination. Even when it comes to art, creativity is no rarity. "Everybody is original. Everybody can design—if not supremely, at least beautifully." So said Henry Wilson, teacher of art teachers.

Imaginative power bears but little relationship to schooling—as illustrated by the story about the Texas cattle raiser who, on seeing an Illinois car approaching his home, dashed to the kitchen and gasped to his houseboy:

"Rastus, a big packer from up North is comin' in. When I was at Chicago, I boasted to him that we have a bull here that races the Sunset Limited 25 miles across our ranch every morning and always wins. The man wanted to see the critter, so now he's here. You've got to handle him. I've gone *away*."

As his master dove through the back door, Rastus went to the front and greeted the visitor with the explanation that his boss had just left for New Orleans—then to Jacksonville and Atlanta—then to New York—then to Toronto—then to Cleveland and Cincinnati on the way to Chicago—then to St. Louis—then to Denver—then to Seattle—then home, after a visit in Hollywood.

"Wow! What a trip! How long before he'll return?"

"Two days."

"Two days! How's he traveling—in a jet plane?"

"No, sah," replied Rastus. "He's ridin' bareback—he's ridin' on that fast-runnin' bull of his."

2.

Psychologists agree that imagination is a gift possessed by all of us. The president of the American Psychological Association recently said: "It is only a layman's idea that the creative person is peculiarly gifted with a certain quality that ordinary people do not have. Creative acts can be expected of almost all individuals."

We differ in creative drive far more than in creative talent. This disparity is apparent even in children. According to Dean Ralph Horn, pupils fall into these three types:

"The Me-Toos: They want to be told what to think. Then they recite it back to you.

"The Get-Alongs: These try to find out what the teachers want, and do just enough work to earn C or D grades.

"The Problem-Solvers: These are the ones who like new ideas, like to spring their ideas in class, and like to get credit for them."

To be a problem-solver we do not have to have the talent of a genius such as Leonardo da Vinci. Called "the most versatile human being who ever lived," he gave birth to thousands of brain children. Many of his ideas were 500 years ahead of his time. They included a self-driven car, various gear combinations and roller bearings, air conditioning, excavating machines, hydraulic tools, airplanes, and even a helicopter. He also created masterpieces of sculpture, painting, music, and architecture.

We should not let a record like that stop us from trying to be more creative in lesser ways. The least we should say to ourselves is that if da Vinci could do that much, surely we can put our creative talent to a greater use than we do.

In the words of Lord Macaulay, the imaginations of most

of us are like "the wings of an ostrich. They enable us to run, though not to soar." But many of us don't even walk. We either stand still creatively, or, worse than that, we slide back from an imaginative childhood into a non-creative adulthood.

"Talent is our affair," said Gustave Flaubert. We can shrivel it through disuse, or we can build it up by practicing creativity—by solving problems, by using our leisure in ways that will exercise our imagination.

3.

A leading psychologist stated that women are inferior to men in "musculation and imagination." I doubt whether this is so. Scientific tests seem to indicate that women have it in them to be as imaginative as men, perhaps more so.

To pose as an analyst of womankind, my only qualifications are six in number—one wife, four daughters, and one secretary. Their minds have long been under the microscope of my hobby. And yet, I confess, they still are mysteries to me.

When our first child came along, I said to my wife: "It's a cinch to bring up a daughter. With my Master's degree in psychology, I'll be able to wind her round my little finger."

How wrong I was she proved to me when she was about 10.

One evening I mildly reprimanded her, only to have her stamp her feet and shriek, "I hate you!" With utmost kindliness (put on, of course, to show off my superior will power) I queried her as to why she hated me. Her reply was the same each time, "Because I hate you"—"because I hate you."

The kindlier and quieter my tone, the more hysterical she became—until finally she was rolling on the floor in a tantrum. I still kept on asking, "Why do you hate me?"

At long last she blurted out, "I *hate* you—because you're so *nice!*"

Despite my inability to comprehend the feminine mind, I may be entitled to the observation that if we men were honest with ourselves, we would recognize that we have no corner on creativity. All we need do is to look into the everyday activities of our womenfolk. Most housewives work their own imaginations far more than most husbands do. A man's job is usually routine, while a woman at home is on her own from dawn to dusk. Just think of the ingenuity she must put into shopping, into planning meals, into prettying up the garden, into rearranging the furniture, into getting her youngsters to do this, and *not* to do that!

Just look at the female stars in the field of creativity—the Edna Ferbers, the Taylor Caldwells, and the countless others. Many husbands have known firsthand how highly creative a woman can be—especially the husbands in the long and brilliant list of creative partnerships made up of married couples.

Admittedly, the record of creative standouts is higher among males than females, as Professor Harvey C. Lehman of Ohio University has shown in his studies. But it is only during the last few minutes of history that women have had a chance to spread their creative wings. As Dr. Paul Popenoe pointed out in his analysis of the psychological differences between sexes, "These differences are acquired rather than inborn, and are visibly diminishing as woman passes to a wider life."

To the extent that mentality has been scientifically analyzed, the evidence proves that creative talent is fairly distributed between sexes. In fact, the Johnson O'Connor Foundation has rated women 25 per cent *more* creative than men.

If there be a difference between sexes, it is probably not in the native talent; it is more likely due to the fact that more men are confronted with more problems to which they are forced to apply creative imagination. And, again, it is that kind of exercise which makes for greater creativity.

4.

Most older people are less creative than younger people —and less creative than they themselves were in earlier years —as a result of the disuse of their imaginative muscles. Although age inevitably saps physical prowess, no law of nature ordains that we must be mentally less creative as we grow older. Physiologists tell us that we can keep on developing our imaginative muscles throughout life. We have it in us to be just as creative at 80 as at 30, according to gerontologist Dr. George Lawton.

Memory necessarily fades with age, and so do other aptitudes. Our creative faculty is about the only inborn ability that can defy Father Time. In this respect, "we are always the same age inside," as Gertrude Stein said.

Those whose jobs are such as to challenge their imaginations all day long find it easier to keep up their creativity. By and large, "they hold up with aging very well," according to Dr. Lawton.

When starting their careers, most of our young people have to perform routine work, and such work tends to dull imagination. Unless they take on other ways to keep their creative wits in trim, they may slip badly before reaching 30. Those whose jobs remain of a routine nature all through life are in ever direr need of creative exercise during their spare time.

Our creative health in adult years is further threatened by the pressures of life. "Introjection" is what psychologists call this cramping effect. Our jobs introject us; our families introject us. Unless we do something to offset this blight, "our creative spirit will retreat so far into the recesses of our being that it may come out as seldom as the ground hog."

Then, too, we face a danger which H. A. Overstreet calls "neophobia." This is the fear which makes oldsters shy away from new ideas. When we hear that Old Man So-and-so is going stale, it usually means that he is suffering from "a dying back of the brain," a loss of creative energy, a paralysis of imagination.

Overdevelopment of judicial judgment is another danger of age. This often carries with it a blinding pride to the effect, "I never make a mistake." Such vainglory tends to blight imagination. Creative effort must always call for guessing; and even the best of guessing cannot avoid error.

5.

Despite all those deterrents, there is plenty of proof that creativity can defy the calendar. One overwhelming mass of evidence is the exhaustive survey of "creative achievement during old age" made by Professor Harvey C. Lehman. This study covered notables who in their day had thought up ideas of importance to the world. Of the 1,000 or more creative achievements listed by Professor Lehman, the median age at which such creativity occurred was 74.

That significant finding fits in with the personal experience of most of us. For example, a competitor of mine went into "retirement" over 30 years ago. Since then, instead of going to seed, he has sown the seed of many a successful venture and of many a worthwhile public service. His name is James Webb Young. At 75 he is more creative than ever. He states most emphatically, "We can keep on growing creatively stronger if we keep on striving to produce ideas."

As a young man I had the privilege of working personally with Herbert N. Casson, and later with Charles F. Kettering —at times when each of them was in his forties. I then looked upon them as ancients.

Kettering did most of his great inventive work long after that. Even up to the age of 75, he kept thinking up ideas right and left. Among other things, he devoted to cancer research the same lively imagination that produced so many engineering innovations.

Herbert Casson kept on sparking until well over 80. During his last 40 years he published a successful magazine. He wrote over 35 books after passing his half-century mark. Incidentally, B. C. Forbes published a 537-page book of quotations "from the best minds of yesterday and today." The most quoted man of all time was Kettering; and Casson ran a close second.

Those men had the advantage of working in creative pursuits. On the other hand, many a person in non-creative work has likewise kept creatively sharp through creative exercise on the outside. One such is Wallace Stevens, poet. For over eight hours every day he devoted himself to a job which called solely for analytic accuracy. Seeking an outlet for creativity, he adopted the hobby of writing verse at home. Winner of the Bollingen Prize in Poetry, his book of poetry caused an outstanding critic to rate him as "the most finished poet of our age."

More and more older people are taking the hobby path to creative alertness. One of the Annual Hobby Shows for Older Persons in New York City comprised over 3,000 separate exhibits. A New York newspaper editorially commented: "This is another proof of the fact that man remains a youth so long as ideas flower in his imagination and can be brought into being by loving craftsmanship."

Another newspaper editor once said, "The function of science is not to add more years to life but to add more life to years." And the one best way in which we can help add more life to our years is everlastingly to "practice the art of creating," as recommended by H. A. Overstreet.

Chapter 3

SOFT ENVIRONMENT makes

it hard to keep creative

O NE REASON WHY we now need to reach out for creative exercise is that our creative growth is inhibited by the very climate in which we live. Sheer necessity forced our forefathers to think up new and better ways of doing things. To keep alive, they had to work their ingenuity overtime. Our softer living numbs our sense of enterprise and deadens our creative spirit.

Although many blame the New Deal for killing the try-hard spirit of yesteryear, its decadence began long before F. D. R. took over. For example, it was over 50 years ago that Newton D. Baker wrote his *Decay of Self-Reliance*. This told of a young man who had asked the war secretary to help him gain admission to Canada in order to trap fur-bearing animals near the Arctic Circle.

"I suppose you think I'm a little crazy, don't you?" asked the young daredevil.

"I wish I could tell you what I really think about you," replied Mr. Baker. "I am wondering whether I do not see in you the last survivor of the pioneer. I wonder whether you are not, in fact, the last young man I shall ever see who is not afraid of the dark and of hardship, and who wants to stand on his own feet and force his own way by the vigor of his own spirit and the strength of his own hands."

Even the cynics will admit that it was the do-or-die philosophy of our forebears which made America so mighty —mighty enough to help support countless foreigners and yet enable 150 million Americans to live better than any people in all history.

Thanks to the toil of scientists, our people now live longer. Physically, we are fitter than ever to work hard and thus *keep* America great. But mentally we are less fit because our minds are so much lazier. Our lethargy is ever aggravated by overdoses of "take-it-easy" narcotics as peddled by those who barter utopian promises in exchange for votes.

We still boast of "free enterprise." But we tend to slur the word *enterprise*—it calls for too much effort and risk. And we tend to glorify *free*—in terms of our freedom to lean on government—in terms of our freedom to loaf on our jobs.

A friend of mine, Rob Roy MacLeod, makes a hobby of history. He has outlined this pattern in the life-cycle of nations: (1) Settlement or conquest, (2) Development of extractive industry, (3) Development of manufacturing, (4) Concentration of population, (5) Increase in tax burden, (6) Diminishment of liberty, (7) Decay of national character, (8) Decline of the nation.

We have passed through the first three of those steps. As to the fourth, 61 per cent of us now live in urban areas, and history indicates that 50 per cent is the danger point.

The fifth step of increased taxation is upon us. We now use one-fourth of our national income to run our government. According to history, the safe maximum is 20 per cent. As to the sixth step, many of our best thinkers are inclined to believe that we are fast forsaking true liberty in favor of false security.

And what about the seventh step? Are we willing to work as hard as our forebears? Are we as honest as they were? Has our personal creativity kept pace with our technological progress?

Henry J. Fuller worked his way through Worcester Tech,

where later he endowed an annual award for the origination of "a useful product or device." Winning ideas in the past have included a bridge, a glider, a lathe, a temperature control, a safety device for a gun, and a shallow-diving outfit. In recent years, interest in the award has sadly fallen off. "Yankee boys are feeling the influence of living under a government where Poppa Knows Best and Poppa Will Provide." That's Bruce Barton's explanation of this apathy.

There are many signs that Yankee ingenuity is on the wane —not because we are born with less creative talent, but because we no longer try hard enough to use the talent that is in us.

2.

The "why try?" creed of so many of us is mirrored in a parody of the 23rd Psalm recently published in *The Memphis Commercial Appeal.* Here's the first line: "The State is my shepherd, I shall not work; it maketh me to lie down on good jobs."

That could be laughed off as the grousing of a cynical editor. But, unfortunately, comprehensive polls reveal that the majority of our people no longer believe that hard work pays. What caused this change? Partly our nation's prosperity— partly our series of wars—partly our political paternalism— partly our parental attitudes.

Our grandfathers strove to make their sons rise early and work late. In our generation, most of us seek to feather-bed our sons.

It used to be that the way to forge ahead was to push harder than the other fellow. In many cases, seniority rights now make it safe to coast.

The fear of losing our jobs used to make us use our brawn and brain to the utmost. Too many of us now lull ourselves with the assurance, "They can't fire me. And if I am laid off, I can still get jobless pay while doing nothing."

The head of a firm of white-collar employees was asked by a business consultant, "How many people have you here?"

"About 500," the employer answered.

"Suppose that tomorrow morning no customers should call, no mail be delivered, no telephone or telegraph messages be received—how many of your people would be able to keep themselves constructively busy?"

The employer was silent for a while. "I am sure of three," he said finally, "and fairly sure of a fourth."

The bigger the business gets, the more likely it is that even the men in management will let their minds loaf. When it comes to creative thinking, many an executive considers it wiser *not* to advance ideas—lest he be classed by his associates as "screwy."

Even among educators the "why try?" philosophy is taking its toll. The head of a midwestern university recently lamented that seniority advancement is crippling the initiative of teachers. "It is even getting so that some of those whom we promote to full professorships virtually retire while still on full salary."

Surely, these are damning indications that our very climate is more and more inimical to creative effort.

3.

As Mark Twain said, "Hunger is the handmaid of genius." It is sad but true that fear of adversity does most to spur creative effort.

Compared to our own past, and compared to other peoples, nearly all of us Americans live on Easy Street. With no wolves at our doors, we tend to let our imaginations go to rust. Prosperity also breeds an overcritical attitude—causes us to look down our noses at those who stick out their necks with ideas. This attitude in turn tends to atrophy our own imaginations.

In my father's day, the fear of a penniless old age drove

many to use their minds to the utmost. But now, those who trustingly look forward to pensions tend to anesthetize their spirit of effort.

From the standpoint of an individual's utilization of his talents, a sense of security is often a hindrance. According to William Feather, "Insecurity is the chief propulsive power in the world." And this truth applies with double force to our creativity.

4.

Group spirit used to encourage those who tried hard. The go-getter was looked up to; the pace-setter was admired. Both are now condemned as anti-social. Competitive spurs have been becoming duller and duller.

A Reuter's dispatch recently told about a welder in England who was fined by his union for working "too hard" in order to earn more money for his family. His fellow workers went even further and had him fired from his job, as a warning to others who might sin in the same way.

Many a merchant who used to be on his creative toes has become flat-footed. Now that goods are scarcer than dollars, salesmen who formerly used their ingenuity at every turn now grow stale for want of creative exercise.

Even in athletics, competitive spirit is not what it was. For example, the best boxers of today do not train as hard as did the old-timers. Who ever heard of a present-day pugilist climbing mountains for exercise? Jim Jeffries made a habit of doing just that.

But Jeffries could keep most of what he earned in the ring, while Joe Louis could never catch up with what he owed his government. Higher and higher taxes are the arch deadeners of incentive in every line of endeavor.

When the Senate was debating the income tax in 1909, a member declared that if Uncle Sam could take one per cent of a citizen's income, he would take 10 per cent or even 50 per cent. To which Senator Borah responded angrily: "Such talk is nonsense. The American people would never stand for a tax of 50 per cent." And now, the income tax rate of some of us reaches as high as 94.5 per cent.

Such incentive killers have made our climate far less conducive to creative effort. This is all the more reason why we as individuals should deliberately go out of our way to take on creative exercise and thus keep our imaginations a-humming—despite Hell and high taxes.

5.

It is likely that 70 per cent of us will be urban dwellers within the near future.

Cities tend to sap imaginative strength in all except the few who work in the arts and in creative phases of business and science. Those in routine jobs practice ingenuity far less than do their country cousins.

Rural life carries with it chores which tend to keep people on their creative toes. A scientific light on this was recently shed by a committee of educators who, with a grant from the Carnegie Foundation, made a five-year survey to determine the geographical origin and the economic backgrounds of those who had made good as creative scientists. In interpreting the committee's findings, *Newsweek* editorially commented: "The conclusion is that creative research is a grass-roots business. . . . It thrives where memories of frontier days still linger. . . . Its adherents come chiefly from the economically lower middle class."

City dwellers have had less need to use their hands and heads to get things done. Most of us have been able to get someone else to fix our plumbing, or repair our car, whereas most ruralites have taken such problems into their own hands.

But this is no longer as true as it was a few years ago. More and more people in the city are doing their own home repairing, remodeling, and redecorating. There are two reasons for this change. One is that it is harder to get that handyman from around the corner to do odd jobs for us. Most plumbers, for example, have enough big work so that they prefer to pass up our little troubles. Many a city householder is thus being forced to use his own ingenuity on his leaky faucet. The other reason for this new trend is expense. Small services which used to cost a pittance now cost too much.

The fact that urban people are doing more and more of their own home repairs is shown by the growing demand for mechanical magazines and the so-called "shelter" books. The circulation of the former group has gone up 230 per cent in the past 10 years. Meanwhile, the shelter books have shown a gain of 149 per cent.

6.

War and fears of war likewise tend to weaken us creatively. The armed services train most of their members to do as they are told rather than to think for themselves.

Then, too, war breeds anti-creative complexes—a feeling of "What's the use?"—a worry that kills concentration and maims effort. The one exception to that rule is creative research. The workers in this field are inspired and spurred by what they do in wartime to hasten peace. Thus, during World War II, our research laboratories turned out new ideas as never before.

That record would not have been possible had those scientists been working in the shadow of personal fear, as were the Germans. Then, too, researchers need free rein, and in this respect we may have a secret weapon as against Russia. In the opinion of Dr. James B. Conant, Sovietized science is doomed to fail—for the reason that the Russians impose a party line on research. They deny and ridicule freedom of enquiry. They have put an end to independent inventors and amateur scientists. "For the short run, the Soviet system can succeed," Dr. Conant said. "But for the long pull, the verdict of history may well be otherwise."

*   *   *

Except for that last point, this chapter has painted a gloomy picture by way of showing how most of our environmental influences are conspiring to stunt our creative growth. Why stress these negatives? Because readers who care about their creativity should recognize the obstacles—should realize that, more than ever before, they need to take on creative exercises, consciously and constantly. Only thus can they keep their imaginations in shape to win life's battles.

Chapter 4

EDUCATION could do more

to develop creativeness

SOME OF US college graduates have long wondered why our schooling all but ignored our one most precious gift, and we are glad that more and more of our educational leaders are likewise questioning our curricula. According to Dr. Oliver Carmichael, an intensive search is under way for a "missing link"—a mysterious lack in our educational process. He reports that "at no time in the history of the country has there been such a stir about the ends and means of education."

"The appalling neglect" of creativity could be one reason for that ferment. The accepted concept of Holism calls for the development of "all aspects of the whole individual"— and yet our educators have seemed to treat imagination as if it were a negligible faculty of the mind, despite overwhelming evidence to the contrary.

Higher education may even tend to stifle creative thinking. College graduates should rate higher than non-college people in scientific tests for creativity, but they don't. Dr. J. P. Guilford reports that the most common complaint he has heard concerning college graduates as researchers is that "while they can do assigned tasks with a show of mastery of the techniques they have learned, they are much too helpless when called upon to solve problems where new paths are demanded." A study by The Brookings Institution confirmed this paradox.

The aims of education are to fill the mind, to drill the mind, and to build character. A well-filled mind is certainly essential to creativity, since facts are the wherewithal of ideas. But grave danger lurks in our memory-stuffing. In his *The Aims of Education*, Alfred North Whitehead warned: "We must beware of what I call 'inert ideas'—ideas that are merely received into the mind without being utilized, or tested, or thrown into fresh combinations." And yet nearly every diploma is based on the intake and retention of relatively dead data.

Even in posing "hypothetical" problems, too many teachers consider them answered only when solved in strict accordance with the text. An original solution, instead of being rewarded, is often penalized.

In its aim to train the mind, education has concentrated on building up judicial judgment—strengthening the critical faculty of the student. When this is carried to extreme it tends to make the student *less* creative. For an overdeveloped discriminative faculty is a natural enemy of imagination.

The same is true of glorifying an "academic attitude." To quote an educator: "Students gradually acquire a spirit of mellow tolerance and scholarly insight, but lose the creative impulse." The fact is that, while generating ideas, we have to keep steamed up with almost irrational enthusiasm—until we verify, and find that we have misfired. According to Charles Kettering, duds are the steppingstones by which we reach worthwhile ideas.

Not only our would-be inventors, but *all* of us, could do with more creative training while at school. Obviously, we cannot count on education to prepare our minds for all the demands of later life. What we need most is that higher order of resourcefulness which only a well-developed imagination can supply.

2.

Educational tradition stresses *critical* intelligence, rather than *creative* intelligence. *"Can it be tested?"* was one of the questions that held back the teaching of creativity. Then, starting in the early 50's, scientific research at several universities produced tests for the identification of creative talent and tests for the developability of creative potential.

Creativity necessarily lacks exactness. And yet it should qualify, as the social sciences do, under the broad definition of *scientia* as "organized knowledge"—as opposed to the narrower definition of science as *"numerically* organized knowledge."

Some of our best educators feel that training in creativity is incompatible with the inculcation of regular habits of study. They erroneously regard effort and imagination as irreconcilable, despite the fact that nearly all leading creativists will attest that effort is the core of origination. This educational misconception may stem from the fact that in a creative process, there must be mysterious pauses—periods of so-called "incubation" in which "illumination" does its subconscious work. A later chapter will explain how such lulls are fructified by effort.

Another deterrent to the teaching of creativity is that "it would take time away from other subjects. There are too many courses as it is." This presents a real problem. For the "proliferation" of courses which Flexner criticized has kept growing ever greater.

But many of those subjects are of but superficial value, whereas nothing could be more basic than training in creative thinking. If some of the fringe courses had to fall by the wayside in order to make room for the study of creativity, wouldn't that be a net gain?

3.

Although there is but little need for cultivation of imagination at the pre-school level, kindergartens are creative hotbeds. On the other hand, elementary and secondary schools have paid almost no attention to creativity, until just recently.

Most of us college graduates can recall hardly anything in our courses that exercised our imaginations. On the other hand, extra-curricular activities often tend to develop creativity. "The most valuable lessons I learned in college were outside the classroom." That was the conclusion which Henry L. Stimson wrote into his autobiography. To which most grads would say "amen."

Why do prospective employers look with favor upon students who have worked their way through school? Because they have proved their determination? Yes. But also because they have built up a better background of usable knowledge and have developed more ingenuity.

A few colleges cultivate creative effort in students by combining practical work programs with academic study. At Antioch, for example, students alternate 10-week sequences in classes with equal periods of employment in industry or other business. During five undergraduate years, an Antioch student will work for as many as seven or eight employers. But even in this program, wouldn't it be better to assign tasks of thinking up ideas while on the job, and thus make a merit of the student's creative activity?

At Blackburn College, practical work is the order of each day. Either by the cash they earn or by the labor they contribute, the students finance 73 per cent of that institution's operating budget. What strenuous exercise—both physical and creative—those Blackburn undergraduates must have received from helping to build two dormitories, a gymnasium, an administrative center, and a house for prexy!

4.

Prior to 1950, courses in creativity were practically unheard of. The big breakthrough came in 1954 when the Air Force R.O.T.C. inaugurated creativity courses on 200 campuses.

Although Hughes Mearns formed a Department of Creative Education at New York University and headed it from 1926 to 1946, this was abandoned when he reached retirement age. The explanation was that no one could be found to fill his shoes.

In 1949 the University of Buffalo installed a course in creative thinking. It engendered such enthusiastic comment from students that enrollment doubled at the second semester. Such courses are now conducted in the evening program and also at the undergraduate level. Scientific research indicates that those who take these courses become substantially more productive of good ideas.

What the students have said about this course reveals how keenly they hunger for, and how deeply they appreciate, this type of education. A woman who had served as a secretary for 12 years testified that the course had inspired her to start a dress shop of her own, and that she had made a go of it by exercising her newly found ability to create ideas. A student who had marital troubles testified that she had thought her way out of her predicament, thanks to the training the course provided.

Their zeal has been attested by the distances traveled. Three of the students made round trips of over 100 miles in order to attend each class. And the instructor invariably found it hard to end each session—so eager was the group to keep on discussing how to generate more and better ideas.

At Schenectady, General Electric has long offered imaginative training through its course in "creative engineering." Between classes, the students are assigned to scientists who have proved themselves exceptionally ingenious. As apprentices to these seniors, the young inventors-to-be learn by *doing*, as well as by listening and observing.

The one college course in creative thinking was conducted by Professor Robert P. Crawford at the University of Nebraska. The testimony of his graduates, many of them journalists, has been consistently enthusiastic.

5.

Our creative growth tends to slow up in our teens. Any higher education that fails to stimulate imagination faces the danger of making "a straight-cut ditch out of a free, meandering brook," as Thoreau warned. In liberal-arts courses, the least that should be done is to make students *conscious* of their latent creative power, and acquaint them with its known principles. There are now many examples of this.

Professional schools, too, have started to teach creativity. At Harvard and elsewhere, students of business administration are being made to realize that creative thinking is vital to the operation of any successful enterprise. Countless case histories demonstrate the role of imagination in industry and commerce. The study of these conditions the minds of the students. The posing of specific problems helps them to sharpen their own creative wits.

Schools of journalism have begun to stress creativity. In the opinion of many publicists, they have overemphasized techniques, despite the fact that *ideas* are the vital ingredients of writing. The School of Journalism at Drake University now requires its students to take a course in creative problem-solving.

Technological education shows a heartening trend toward emphasis on imagination. More and more scientists concur in Dr. James B. Conant's contention that "apart from thoroughness and accuracy, the essence of research of any kind is *imagination.*"

Admiral Luis de Florez gained fame as the prime developer of the Navy's Special Training Division during the last war. Here's his testimony: "Just as the habit does not make the monk, neither does the certificate make the engineer. Some spark of originality, some creative spirit, must be added to technical training to achieve the result. All the extraordinary fruits of modern engineering, at our every hand, have resulted from creative thinking based on original concepts, using past experience and past accomplishments only as guides."

Most engineering colleges are now combining general enlightenment with technical training. Their curricula call for solutions of problems rather than memorization of data. But as yet, no curriculum goes half as far to develop creativity as does the course conducted by General Electric.

And how about law schools? Nearly all legal lights attest that resourcefulness wins more cases than does knowledge of Blackstone. And theological schools—even they have begun to teach creativity. Obviously, the more creative a pastor becomes, the better he can lead his flock. The same is true of teachers' colleges. All educators agree that the imaginative teacher is usually the better teacher.

6.

Far more creative thinking could be put into college courses without adding a single subject. Take history, for example. If teachers would only show how ideas have *made* history, they could teach that subject better, and could incidentally stimulate the imagination of their students. In 1958, the University of Buffalo conducted a conference of history teachers. The 70 participants produced 540 ideas for teaching history more creatively.

History professors might even pose such problems as "What would have happened if America had not been discovered until the 19th century?" . . . "What would have

happened if Hitler had made peace with England?" . . .
"Would China have been less likely to stall a Korean armistice if MacArthur had not been fired?" The brainstorming of such problems would require original syntheses from known facts and would thus provide creative exercise.

Most obviously, the teaching of psychology should include creativity. Students are usually offered a bewildering array of sub-courses, such as physiological, abnormal, applied, educational, genetic, social, child, religious, and animal psychology—to name only a few. A sub-course in creative imagination could do much to strengthen the students' ability. The University of Minnesota has pioneered this type of teaching.

Any course in creativity should call for active participation by students. The best sessions would be seminars— workshops in which all present would strive to generate ideas of their own, right then and there.

That type of learning is in line with the trend which we non-educators applaud. We agree with Harold Rugg and James Wendenhall of Columbia in their belief that education should employ "every possible agency to stimulate the active participation of the pupil." According to these co-authors, "The active school is replacing the listening school" —and this is a cheering prospect.

In every attempt at creative teaching, students should be assigned outside projects of their own. Classroom discussion does not do enough to activate the "type of thinking" which Admiral de Florez advocates—"The kind which must color our work in later life and provide the basis for creative accomplishment." Nor does it promote "the exercise of mental functions in the manner in which they will be called upon to perform in our life's work."

7.

An editor whose views are highly respected by teachers agreed that education should pay more attention to creativity. But he asked, "Can it be taught?" . . . "Is there enough substance to teach?" . . . "Are there teachers who can teach it?"

To the extent that there is substance in the workings and the powers of the human mind, there is plenty of teachable substance—far more so than in philosophy, for instance. The creative principles are known. Some techniques, although empirical, are workable. But even greater than this pedagogical substance is the limitless subjective substance. For if and when a student is "introduced" to his own creative power, he will find his own mind to be an ever-widening source of self-revelation.

As to who can teach creativity, Alfred North Whitehead put his finger on this problem. "Imagination," he wrote, "is a contagious disease. It cannot be measured by the yard, or weighed by the pound, and then delivered to the students by members of the faculty. It can only be communicated by a faculty whose members themselves wear their learning with imagination."

The problem of training teachers to teach creativity is a real hurdle. But our country has never been stopped by such obstacles. If there *is* an "appalling" need for the teaching of creativity, we should be ingenious enough to find, and to train, men and women who can teach it. If we wait until we have teachers who are "creativists"—relatively as skilled as botanists or biologists—we shall never make a start. For how can we gain enough experience to teach such teachers unless we first make a serious stab at teaching creativity?

In the past few years, the inauguration of so many courses in creativity has provided the experience on which to base sound answers to the questions of what to teach and how best to teach it. And, at last, adequate teaching tools are now available in the form of textbooks, instructor's manuals and student workbooks. The further advancement of the creative education movement will largely depend on the supply of educators who are able and eager to teach creativity.

Fortunately, the teaching profession has come to realize the need for the development of creativity. For example, a 1964 report of the American Association of University Professors starts with these words: "The basic functions of a college or university are to preserve, augment, criticize and transmit knowledge—*and to foster creative capacities.*" (The italics are mine.)

Thus it seems likely that education will eventually help fill the gap caused by the loss of those environmental influences which formerly forced us to keep creatively strong. Meanwhile it behooves all of us to take on creative exercises of our own and thus enhance our creative ability through practice.

Chapter 5

EXERCISE can build up minds

as well as bodies

THE CHAPTER AFTER this will start spelling out the creative exercises which are good for us, and enjoyable to-boot. But since some may doubt the value of exercise, let's first take a look at this question. "I get my exercise acting as pallbearer to my friends who exercise." Although Chauncey Depew said this with his tongue in his cheek, he was sincerely skeptical.

The other extreme is that "practice makes perfect," or as Periander said in 590 B.C., "Practice is everything." Ralph Waldo Emerson toned that down a bit, but still held that "practice is nine-tenths."

All we claim here is that in our fight to keep and to build up our creative power, exercise is more than half the battle.

When it comes to physical skills, there can be no doubt about the value of practice. For instance, I recently saw a juggler keeping six balls in the air while standing on one foot, poised on a tightrope 20 feet above a hard floor. Even a cat couldn't do that without spending at least one of his lives on practice.

Constant drill in physical skills can even defy superannuation. Television recently featured a spirited performance of clog dancing by Billy Hess, 76 years old and still going strong. If he had not kept up his practice, his feet would have lost their timing long since.

Likewise in golf. A friend who won a championship in his 20's now finds it hard to break 100. Another friend, Johnny Smith, never hit a golf ball until he was 40; but at 66 he could shoot in the low 70's. He will tell you that practice made him the low scorer that he is.

At the age of 19, Willie Hoppe won his first billiard championship. At 63 he was still unbeatable. In the past 50 years he put in more than 70,000 hours of practice, and he practiced four hours every day.

One great good of exercise is that it makes the use of our strengths more spontaneous in an emergency. I found this out to my delight one rainy night last winter. Leaving my New York office on that black evening, I made sure that the light was with me before crossing Madison Avenue.

Halfway across, a truck came zooming toward me. I had no choice. If I stopped, I was done for. If I kept going, I might escape death. So I dashed. I never got off to a faster start, even while on my college track team.

The fender of the truck struck my coattail as I brushed by. Standing breathless on the curb, I thanked my lucky stars that I had always kept my legs in shape through constant exercise.

Without warning, life has a way of plunging us into crises that call for creative agility—just as that near-miss called for physical agility. If we keep our mental muscles supple, we are more likely to think creatively enough, and *fast* enough, to meet such emergencies.

2.

Was James Russell Lowell right when he proclaimed, "*Exercise* is good for the muscles of the mind?" Discussing this issue, Dr. L. L. Thurstone of the University of Chicago has said:

"One of the most common questions about primary abilities is whether they can be trained; the answer is in the affirmative." He went on to state that although the more gifted naturally profit more from practice than the less gifted, everybody can improve his mental skills through exercise.

As a rule a person low in creative talent would never catch up with a more gifted colleague, even if both had equal exercise. On the other hand, some of us get off to slower starts —our talents are late in flowering. Many a slow-starter has risen to creative heights, even after 40.

Teachers know from experience that there are slow-burners as well as boy wonders—and that even the kind of talent a pupil may develop is often unpredictable. One educator confessed that a boy he had labeled as clumsy turned out to be a speed artist in major-league baseball; a lad he had classed as cowardly later won a medal for courage; a lass who "wasted her time" doodling eventually distinguished herself as a painter; a petty pilferer grew to be the treasurer of a university; a blasphemer became a man of God. Yes, we can change; and exercise can do much to direct and empower our transformations.

Scientific testers have fixed upon 17 "known aptitudes" of which 12 are entirely mental and five are partly physical. The traits of tonal memory, pitch discrimination, and eye dominance, are so inborn that they cannot be acquired. All 14 of the other aptitudes, however, can be developed by practice.

3.

When it comes to specific skills of the mind, the good of exercise has been quite conclusively proved. As Dr. Albert Edward Wiggam has pointed out, "By practicing mental arithmetic 20 minutes a day for 20 days, adults can more than double their ability to calculate. By the same token, creative exercise can regain for us much of the imaginative power we have lost through neglect."

As to the effect of exercise on memory, Dr. Donald Laird has proved that we can almost double our power of recall. Robert H. Nutt, who has trained the memories of over 60,000 people, has this to say: "In all my 14 years of teaching, I have met very few individuals who possess a naturally good memory." Bruno Furst claims that it's no accident that Jim Farley can greet thousands of people by name, or that John Kieran can carry in his head a veritable encyclopedia of information. "You, too, can be a Farley, a Kieran," in Furst's opinion, "if you're willing to go to the same trouble. Anyone who wishes to acquire a reliable memory should devote from 15 minutes to half an hour daily to mental setting-up exercises."

I have often been awed by the memory of waiters in the Colonial Room of the Hotel Roosevelt, where I have breakfasted hundreds of times. After I had absented myself from there for over three years, headwaiter Henry May welcomed me back early one winter morning with this greeting: "Good morning, Mr. Osborn. Would you like the same as usual—double orange juice, half a grapefruit, bacon and eggs, dry toast, and coffee?"

"Yes," said I, "and what a marvelous memory you have!"

"Thank you," replied Henry. Then he added: "Oh, yes, you like your bacon medium but slightly scorched on the edges, don't you?"

Bill Feather remarked on this mastery of memory as built up by constant practice: "A cab driver did a short drive for me, and when I paid him off, he remarked that he hadn't had me as a passenger for three years. He named the location of the spot where he had driven me. It was a dwelling in a respectable neighborhood, thank you."

Adolf Hitler practiced like mad to outshine all of his cohorts in the ability to remember. When a field commander complained that he could not hold a certain sector, Der Fuehrer demanded that he recite all details as to ordnance, ammunition, vehicles, planes, and manpower on his battlefront. When the general hesitated, Hitler rattled off the precise statistics and then scolded him for his stupidity.

Exercise can certainly put life into memory. And it can do likewise for creative imagination.

4.

A basic difference in personality is that some of us are objective and others are subjective—some think outwardly, and in terms of others; others think inwardly, in terms of themselves.

The human engineers seem to feel that creativity more often goes with subjectivity than with objectivity. This is probably so in most cases; but still there is no reason to believe that if we are subjective at 20, we have to remain that way the rest of our lives. By the right kind of exercise, we can make ourselves more creative, and yet grow less and less subjective. I have seen living proofs of how men have changed their abilities and their personalities in just that way.

Without doubt a survey of countless disciples of Dale Carnegie would factually demonstrate that, through his coaching and their own efforts, they have done much to slough off subjectivity and take on objectivity.

5.

Even distinctly emotional traits can be changed by exercise. The more we practice kindness, the kinder we become. By practicing good cheer we become cheerier ourselves. And we certainly can develop spiritual power by exercises such as saying prayers, reading the Bible, and going to church.

As proof that exercise can likewise build up will power, there are countless cases in the records of Alcoholics Anonymous. And the many of us who have read Henry Morton Robinson's *The Cardinal* will know how practice can put steel into a man's backbone.

Even a sense of humor can be developed by training. The University of Florida tried out a course to prove that this was so. It worked; and that course is now a permanent part of that institution's curriculum.

By practice we can even make ourselves more modest or more immodest. Through my years of intimate association with Alexander Woollcott I observed firsthand how he changed himself in this respect. In an even more spectacular way, George Bernard Shaw did the same. After Shaw's death, his friend Bertrand Russell reported:

"When I first knew him (1896) his shyness was still obvious. He came to my flat on one occasion to read a new play of his to about 20 friends. He was pale and trembling with stage fright, in spite of the audience being so small and well-disposed." Just think what a change G.B.S. wrought in himself! By practicing his barbed wit, he supplanted humility with arrogance.

As John Powers, Harry Conover, and other charm trainers have demonstrated, even enthusiasm can be developed by exercise. Elmer Wheeler has added further proof through his teaching of salesmanship. And so has many a football coach. In his *Try Giving Yourself Away*, David Dunn showed how, even in those to whom it does not come naturally, enthusiasm can be cultivated.

6.

As to what exercise can do for imagination, let's go back to where we started and realize that our creativity tends to ebb early in life unless we do something to keep it flowing. Let's accept the truth laid down by Edward Gibbon: "All that is human must retrograde if it does not advance."

If there is any doubt about the value of creative exercise, the question should be, not whether exercise can keep us from slipping creatively, but whether it can make us imaginatively stronger and stronger.

To this latter end we must admit that the more strenuously we go at it, the better. When Shakespeare referred to "the rich advantage of good exercise," he indicated that practice varies in degrees of value. Best of all, of course, is actual *doing*—the actual combining of effort with imagination. Thus creative power can be retained or regained—and "it can actually be stimulated into growth," to use the words of H. A. Overstreet.

But to go from strength to strength we need, in addition to practice, some knowledge of how our creative mind works. For that reason another chapter will outline what is generally believed to be the *modus operandi* of creativity. The need of such understanding was recently brought out by Dr. Guilford: "I believe that much can be done to encourage the development of creativity. This development might be in the nature of actual strengthening of the functions involved or it might mean the better utilization of what resources the individual possesses, or both. In any case, a knowledge of the functions is important."

Those in non-creative jobs have to face the problem of summoning up enough effort to keep imagination in training. Many a man would willingly take on herculean measures to save his hair, and yet would turn his back on such creative exercises as would help save him from mental baldness.

William James urged: "Keep the faculty of effort alive in you by a little gratuitous exercise every day." And what better way to practice effort than to practice creativity? By picking a problem and pitting our mind against it, we invigorate our will. For, as Edmund Burke said, "He that wrestles with us strengthens our nerves and sharpens our skill. Our antagonist is our helper."

7.

Although the best of creative exercise calls for effort, even that can be fun—as we will see when we scan the different forms of exercise. For one thing, most of these activities provide a change; and a change is often pleasurable, as Winston Churchill pointed out in his *Painting As a Pastime*:

"It is no use saying to the tired 'mental muscles'—if one may coin such an expression—'I will give you a good rest,' 'I will go for a long walk,' or 'I will lie down and think of nothing.' The mind keeps busy just the same. If it has been worrying, it goes on worrying. It is only when new cells are called into activity, when new stars become the lords of the ascendant, that relief, repose, refreshment are afforded."

The recreative effect of creative effort was also pointed up by Gardner Hunting: "Human beings find less rest in idleness than in a change of occupation. If you scoff at the idea, just try it. Instead of collapsing in an easy chair, try tackling your hobby. Or write that neglected letter, or help Johnny to build that radio receiving set. Activity—especially creative activity—is far better recreation than loafing."

*　　*　　*

Up to this point we have tried to prove that: (1) Imagination is important. (2) All of us possess this gift. (3) It tends to wane with adulthood. (4) We cannot count on education or environment to keep it strong. (5) Exercise can help us not only to retain this talent, but also to build it up.

So now we come to scores of ways in which we can put imagination through its paces—to our everlasting benefit, and to our concurrent enjoyment.

Chapter 6

LITTLE CHILDREN can help

enliven our imagination

"IF I DIDN'T have to bring up children, I could do something to improve my mind." Let's not say that. Let's realize, instead, that we can do a lot for our mentalities by being with children, and by caring for children—*if* we go at it creatively.

In my experience, children between four and 12 provide us with the most worthwhile creative thinking. Their minds churn with curiosity as well as imagery. Their make-believe and their ingenuity can help make our creative blood run red.

Teen-agers, on the other hand, are less likely to be creatively radiant. Not all of them, of course. But, by and large, we adults can do more to brighten our imagination by basking in the sunshine of minds not yet beclouded by adolescence.

2.

Merely being with children can tone up our creativity. Dr. Albert G. Butzer cites his call on a couple expecting a new arrival. Their two-year-old informed him that the new baby would arrive by air from Tenafly, where the family formerly lived, and that the plane would circle over the house and deposit the baby on the front lawn. "He carried me along on that flight," related Dr. Butzer. "He gave my imagination a real lift."

A newspaper woman, Jean Rindge, claims that her imagination is kept alert by her three-year-old son, who has a fictional buddy named "Wow." Asked to describe Wow, he said: "Wow is like a light. He looks like a chicken. He smiles at your legs."

The unexpected interests of little ones tend to lift our minds out of ruts. A week after a young father had shown his little son the World's Fair at New York, he asked the boy what he liked best of what he saw. Said the boy: "The horse made of prunes and the picture of the sick monkey." Similarly, after I had given my 10-year-old son a day in New York—visiting Ripley's Odditorium and introducing him to Ripley himself, then taking him to a broadcast in Radio City and blowing him to a lobster dinner on Broadway —I asked him at bedtime what had impressed him most. Said he, "That view of Venus we had for 10 cents through the big telescope on 42nd Street."

A young associate of mine, Ted Higinbotham, told me about his little girl: "She had an invisible friend around our summer cottage. He is named Ignac. If we say, 'Where's Ignac?' she says: 'Outside.' When we ask, 'What is Ignac doing now?' her answers are always different—depending on whether at that moment Ignac is a dog, a boy, a monkey, a turkey, or some other creature."

Similarly, a little boy next door to us has a lion named Bobo living in his hedge. We have lots of fun keeping our cocker spaniel safe from Bobo. And my own little son used to have an imaginary friend named Dr. Renschler. Often at table, when the conversation dulled, he would quote Dr. Renschler; then he would go off into gales of laughter, and take us with him.

A mother on our street prides herself on her imagination; but she is no match for her little ones. On each evening during the week before last Christmas, she had her eight-year-old son and five-year-old daughter enact a scene from the Nativity story—the boy playing Joseph; the girl, Mary. On Christmas Eve the lad came in wearing his Hopalong Cassidy outfit. In the middle of the play he whipped out his six-shooter, "made like" shots, then yelled: "Okay, Mary! I got Herod."

Sometimes these flights of fancy are puzzling. A friend of mine found that his Waring Blendor had come to be the motor of a Russian plane to his three-year-old, and that the outdoor swing had become a Russian jet in which she could zoom—despite the fact that her folks had never talked about Russia in her presence. And then, when her father asked her if she wouldn't rather ride in an American plane, she answered: "Forty-five." This was the code she had invented to mean "I don't know."

3.

The downright ingenuity of youngsters can set a creative pace for us elders. One evening my nine-year-old grandson surprised me with this one: "Doesn't everybody think all the time?" I tried to explain that real thinking is not just letting one's mind meander, but means applying oneself to a problem and purposively thinking through a solution. That night at bedtime, he called me. "Look," he said. "I broke two of my lead soldiers. Here's how I mended them." Then he showed me how he had fixed them with Scotch tape—a use the manufacturer had never thought of.

When Grace Manney asked our staff to test pie against pie, I turned over my two sample mixes to my oldest daughter. She baked the two pies and marked each whole one with an A and a B for identification. But her nine-year-old Teddy insisted that not only the pies, but each cut, should be identified. So, using toothpicks for poles and colored paper for pennants, he made flags which marked each piece of pie as either A or B.

Adults whose professions constantly expose them to children offer living proof that grown-ups can grow in imagination as a result of working with little ones. Nearly all the pediatricians I have known have been unusually bright of mind, partially because of that fact. Teachers of kindergartners and of lower grades are likewise creative to an exceptional degree. Aptitude testers report that 58 per cent of them rate A in imagination—an extraordinarily high rating compared to other occupational groups. This is one of many proofs that contact with the young tends to keep our imaginations young.

4.

To get the most creative help from children, we must meet them more than halfway; we must let ourselves go; we must throw dignity to the winds. Little ones have often referred to me as "silly"; and I have taken this as a compliment. I am glad that they like to play with me—to make me prance around on all fours and pretend that I am a horse—to make me do other didoes which other adults might deem beneath their dignity.

Proudly I confess that I have *not* "put away childish things"—that I *like* to get in tune with childish moods. Because I am that way, I believe that I have profited creatively from my juvenile contacts. And how I have loved it!

I know many other fathers who feel the same way. One of them is a next-door neighbor, one of the nation's legal lights. Many a summer evening, sitting on my front lawn, I have eavesdropped on this mature man as he dined with his eight-year-old, his four-year-old, and his wife.

Such silliness! He chimes in with his little ones as they let their fancies fly. He even leads them into flights of fantasy more childish than their own. And never a chiding word from his wife. She understands. She had been a brilliant teacher in a truly progressive school before she married this supposedly starchy member of the bar.

And I understand. So much so that when the Senate, in June 1951, confirmed Robert Millonzi as U. S. Security Exchange Commissioner, I felt sure that one reason for his selection was that he combines creative power with his legal knowledge—and that his little ones had helped a lot to keep that imagination of his in the pink.

Luckily, present-day fathers are less afraid to unbend than were their forebears. But even in former days there were notable exceptions, as illustrated by an unpublished story told to me by a personal friend of mine, Edward Michael, then 101 years of age. His own eyes saw Abraham Lincoln unbend so far as to play leapfrog after his election as President of the United States.

On that Sunday in 1861 Lincoln was on his way to Washington to be inaugurated. He was bowed down by the heaviest problem that had ever confronted a President—the secession of the South had begun the day before. He and Mrs. Lincoln went to church that morning, leaving young Michael and young Todd Lincoln at play in the hotel attic. On returning from worship, Father Abe went upstairs to see what the lads were up to. He found them playing leapfrog and joined in the game himself.

Dignity in its finest sense was personified by Christ. And yet He could always commune with children. As Bruce Barton wrote in *The Man Nobody Knows*: "Wherever He went the children flocked. . . . They swarmed around, climbing on His knees, tugging at His garments, smiling up into His eyes, begging to hear more of His stories. . . . It was all highly improper and wasteful in the eyes of His disciples. With bustling efficiency they hastened to remind Him that He had important appointments. They even tried to push the eager mothers back."

But Jesus would have none of it. "Suffer little children to come unto Me!" He commanded. And He added one of those sayings which should make so clear the message of His gospel. "They are the very essence of the Kingdom of Heaven. Unless you become like them you shall in no wise enter in." Like them—like little children—laughing, unaffected, trusting, curious and imaginative.

5.

Whether we are bored or stimulated by children largely determines the creative good they do us. Our attitude must never be condescending. Dr. Rudolf Flesch warns: "If you try to talk down to children, they will quickly find you out and shut you up. But if you can take the anchor off your adult imagination—what a wonderful realm you enter with them!"

E. J. Hardy denounced as "stupid" the saying that "little people should be seen and not heard." We should even indulge their whims, according to James Barrie. He believed that "Genius is the power to be a boy again at will." When the statue of Peter Pan was erected in London, he contrived to have it done at night so that the little ones might think it had been put up by the fairies.

Above all, we must be careful not to cramp a child's creative spontaneity. Too many adults exert a petrifying influence upon the young. Many a teacher has seen the intrusion of an alien adult suddenly transform groups of children from highly intelligent artists into clumsy stupids.

How to tell foolishness from genius is a challenge to our grown-up judgment. A little boy may be fooling with tools and wire. Should we order him to stop and start practicing his piano lesson? If so, we may be snuffing the flame of a potential Edison. The puniest effort of a child to try his creative wings should be praised rather than censured—if we recognize the truth that imagination is mankind's most precious gift.

But we need do more than merely encourage our little ones if they are to do us the most creative good. We need to take part with them. We need to play *with* them. The National Recreation Association has conducted a nation-wide program for teaching parents to do just that.

Many teachers have devised play ideas for tots. Caroline Horowitz has thought up 80 such. So far so good. But we parents can get more creative exercise by thinking up play ideas of our own. To avoid sending his little son to dancing school, Carl Ewald, the author, collaborated with him in inventing original dances. Among the many was a warrior dance, a spear dance, a mitten dance and a comic dance dramatizing their mutual distaste for licorice. Both the boy and his dad had fun; and both profited creatively.

An Army captain and his eight-year-old daughter thought up a game called "Face Talk," a secret language in which they acted out each letter by a special grimace. It was so secretive that they could play it without detection, even under the noses of family and friends. What a comradeship that engendered! And what creative exercise it was for both father and child to think up a game like that!

Let's pretend, or, rather, let's co-pretend—as does my stately neighbor with her young Steve. The other evening, while taking a walk, he first noticed their shadows and then started jumping on hers. She jumped on his and they glee-fully kept this up until both of their shadows climbed up a telegraph pole and vanished. Steve was then ready to go home and right to bed.

My young associate Earl Obermeyer used his imagina-tion at home when dining with his four-year-old Marilyn. They pretended they were eating out at his club. They talked across tables to other members and to some of her own little friends. Just another game, another form of participation—good fun and good creative exercise for parent and child.

6.

Let them ask questions, all they want. "What makes knots in wood?" "Why is a raindrop round?" "What holds the stars up?" These questions cultivate curiosity and thereby aid the imagination of both the askers and the answerers.

Sometimes the queries are unanswerable posers, such as the one with which a little boy stumped me while we drove through the country. "What are those strings for?" he asked, pointing to the ropes hanging over a railroad track at either side of a bridge. I explained that if a man were standing on top of a freight car, the ropes would warn him in time to duck before he was knocked off by the viaduct. "Who thought that up?" he demanded. I didn't know then, and I have yet to find out.

Curiosity is an important adjunct to creativity, but effort is its essence. Therefore, to keep our imaginative muscles in trim we must do more than just jog along with our children. We must put in some creative exertion of our own. For instance, instead of reading stories to our young, why not make them up?

Dr. Charles Lutwidge Dodgson transformed himself into the famous Lewis Carroll of *Alice in Wonderland* by thinking up tales to tell his little friends. In similar fashion, a young associate of mine has been growing creatively stronger by making up stories for his three children. He has created a cast of characters in the animal kingdom which undergo adventures far more exciting than could be found in any child's book he could buy.

Still another young associate of mine enthralls his youngest at bedtime with stories based on incidents from her own experiences. Sometimes he even improvises going-to-bed tunes and lyrics, such as, "This is the way I get undressed, get undressed, get undressed," and so on. This gets the child happily tucked in, and it helps sharpen his own creative wits.

Another young father induces his three-year-old to down her cereal by making a game of it. Each spoonful is part of a freight train—first, the engine, then the coal tender, then the horse car. The last spoonful is the caboose. If a gobbet is still left, that's "the switchman's lantern."

Thinking up ways to outwit our children is likewise good creative practice. One pair of parents have made a culprit of the kitchen clock. *They* are not to blame when they have to issue orders. The tyrant is that cruel old clock which insists on calling time for this or that.

The same parents teach orderliness by pretending stupidity. When their only child balks at putting her toys away, they make believe that they are her little brother and sister—trying to "help" her, but clumsily putting each plaything into the wrong place. That arouses the child to see to it that everything is back where it should be.

7.

To get the optimum tonic out of contact with youngsters it is often best to take on one child at a time. An uncle who often entertained both of his nephews on week ends never realized how much the boys could mean to him until he started to have each one come alone, on alternate visits. Try it yourself. Take a small boy on a tramp through the woods. Be a boy with him and you will find your imagination will glow all the way.

Then, too, there is a certain part of the day when a child can best give wings to your mind. It is the going-to-bed time—the mystic period described by Longfellow as "the Children's Hour." It is an event no parent should ever miss.

One young couple told me how their three-year-old daughter rises to heights of fancy at bedtime. The father reports this dialogue as typical of almost every evening:

"What are you going to dream about tonight?"

"Monkeys."

"What will the monkeys be doing?"

"Sitting in a tree, talkin' to me."

"What will they talk to you about?"

"Harry, Bobby, Marcy, Kathy, Ellen, Peter, Donnie,

Davie, Jane and Linda" (naming her little cousins, always in the same order).

After months of that same rigmarole, she added a new touch: "Daddy, hold my hand and come with me to see the monkeys." So now her father has to take her hand in his before she goes to sleep; and, in the morning, he has to tell her what the two of them did with the monkeys during the night.

Monkeydoodle? Perhaps. But that young man is growing creatively stronger week by week. I know, because he is one of our creative staff. And his nightly communion with that little girl is helping him to keep his imagination in high gear.

A little boy sprung these lines on his mother at bedtime: "Do you know what the stars are for? They're the lights which God hangs out so I won't be afraid of the dark."

The radiance of such imaginings can't fail to brighten our minds. At the same time, by actively exercising our creative faculties in thinking up ideas for amusing and training our young, we can do a lot for our creative souls.

So, tomorrow, when you open the door of that beloved bedroom, you might well greet your little one in these words: "Good morning, *teacher*!"

Chapter 7

READING – how to go at it

creatively

A S FRANCIS BACON declared, "Reading maketh a full man." It supplies bread for imagination to feed on, and bones for it to chew upon. But to get the most out of this pastime, we should pick and choose *what* to read.

If we were to peruse every word of every Sunday edition of *The New York Times,* we could spend every waking minute of our lives doing only that—and creatively die in the meantime. We must be selective; and a good test as to what to read might well be this simple question: "How good an exercise for my creative mind will this provide?"

2.

Amazingly few people read books. Columbia University recently found that only 52 per cent of us adults ever open one after we leave school. At the opposite pole is the literary glutton who told Haldeman-Julius that he had read 189 books in as many days.

Our imaginations are whetted by the right kind of fiction, such as that written by Dickens, Dumas, Conrad, and Kipling. Most of the lesser novels, however, prove but little more than vicarious escapes.

The better mysteries can give us good creative workouts

—especially if we read them as if we were participants rather than spectators. On this point, here's the comment of Julian Trivers, a department-store executive in Atlanta: "I stop as soon as the clues are in hand, and then try to think out 'who done it.' I believe that the reason why so many successful thinkers enjoy detective stories is that they like to think up the pay-off in advance. When we *consciously* try to do that, we can't help but flex our imaginative muscles."

Children's books are rich in imagination. A child's reader entitled *Pages of Adventure* is a gold mine of creativity. And did you ever treat your imagination to that uproarious little classic, *Over A Million Cats?* Kipling's juvenile stories can likewise give us a mental glow, especially when we read them aloud to little ones.

A short story is short mainly because it leaves so much to imagination. A young friend of mine named Halbak sold his first short story to a national magazine. "When it was published," he told me, "I asked the editor why my final paragraph had been deleted, and he explained: 'You were just spelling it out. Leave something for the reader to do. Make them use their own imaginations.'"

To gain the most creative exercise from a short story we might well try to outwit the author by reading the first half, then thinking up and writing down our own outline for the latter half. Or let's take a masterpiece by O. Henry and read it almost through. Let's stop at that point and jot down as many different dénouements as we can invent. By thus emulating O. Henry's snap-the-whip endings we can provide our imaginations with sprinting practice.

3.

"The most rewarding form of reading is biography," in the judgment of Harry Emerson Fosdick. Any life worth publishing can't fail to reveal an inspiring record of ideation.

Dr. Albert G. Butzer believes in the Bible as a source of

creative development for those who read it right: "Take the opening chapter, for example. To read this as prose is to miss its magnificence. We should read it as poetry, letting our imaginations linger over one verse after another.

"Or take the incidents in the life of Jesus—stilling the storm on the Sea of Galilee, holding little children in His arms, praying in Gethsemane, dying on the cross. Many such events in Christ's life can come alive to us in all their original vividness if we read of them with our imaginations as well as with our eyes."

William Lyon Phelps likewise recommended Bible-reading. Said he: "I thoroughly believe in a university education for men and women, but I believe a knowledge of the Bible without a college course is more valuable than a college course without the Bible."

During my 30 years of partnership with Bruce Barton, I have often wondered how much of his high creativity came from the way he reads his Bible. In his preface to *The Man Nobody Knows*, he explained *how* he read about Jesus "as though He were a new historical character, about whom I had never heard anything at all." Thus Bruce Barton puts imagination into all his reading.

Certain books on thinking can contribute to our creative development. The list of books in the front of this volume mentions some of the works which can enlighten our understanding and enliven our imagination.

4.

As to periodicals, newspapers carry many features that can quicken our creative spirit. And the fresh facts they convey are rich in creative ore. Middlebury College recognizes this truth. A daughter of mine attending there is now reading a newspaper (other than comics) for the first time in her life. A subscription to *The New York Times* is included in her tuition fees.

Among the general periodicals, *The Reader's Digest* is recommended by Walt Disney in these words: "Your imagination may be creaky or timid or dwarfed or frozen at the joints. *The Reader's Digest* can serve as a gymnasium for its training." Another periodical I find similarly stimulating is a little non-profit magazine called *Guideposts*.

Travel magazines like *National Geographic* and *Holiday* help fill the fuel tanks of our imagination. Women's magazines not only do that for their readers but often run articles which inspire creative effort.

Periodicals like *Popular Science* provide a creative atmosphere, and serve as showcases for new ideas. The fact that these innovations have been thought up by average people tends to give readers more confidence in their own inventive ability.

Certain features in certain magazines have specifically called for creative effort. One such was entitled "Why Don't They?" This presented ideas thought up by ordinary housewives and husbands. Best of all was a feature called "What Would You Have Done?" This set forth a practical problem and a specific solution. For example, here's one contributed by H. N. Broyles:

"While contemplating a rush inventory in a large warehouse, I found myself faced with the job of counting some thousands of coal buckets. These buckets covered an area equal to several large rooms, and were piled in stacks of 24 buckets each. If the stacks had been arranged in regular rows, the task would have been fairly simple. As it was, the stacks were pushed together in an irregular mass.

"It was impossible to walk over the buckets to count the stacks, and there wasn't quite enough time to rehandle and restack them for counting. Yet I got the merchandise counted in about half an hour without touching a single bucket. Can you guess the method I used?"

It would do our imaginative muscles no good to read the solution before first trying to crack the nut with our own teeth. That's why I make a habit of writing down as many alternative solutions as I can think up in 15 minutes. And then I pick out the best of these before looking up the answer.

What was the most likely idea I arrived at in the case set forth above? My plan was to procure a long bamboo pole and a pile of 50 full-page sheets from old newspapers—then, while standing on a ladder, I would impale a page on the end of my rod and stick it over the top of each stack—then I would count up how many sheets I had thus used, and so would arrive at the total tally.

Broyle's own solution was a far better idea: "I got a camera and flash bulb and mounted a tall ladder. From the top I took a picture of the massed buckets. Two prints of the picture were made, and these were given to two clerks. They carefully counted the stacks in the picture, using a sharp pencil to dot each stack as it was counted. When the two counts tallied, we knew we had the correct figure."

About 1700 trade journals cover practically all lines of human activity. They feature new and better methods of making things or performing services. Many of these periodicals do much to stimulate imagination.

Variety is the weekly bible of those who work in movies, broadcasting, television, music and in the theatre. It teems with ideas thought up by people who practice creativity day and night. Its very language rubs the reader's imagination with a coarse towel. "Aqua Follies Sock 110,000 in Seattle." That was the headline on this capsule dispatch: "Seattle's unique Aqua Theatre, seating 5,243, got its initiation Aug. 11–20 with 'Aqua Follies.' Sellouts for night performances were the rule, with some standees, for a smash $110,000. House was scaled from $3.50."

It may even be that the reading of advertisements can be good for imagination. Each ad is crammed with the best creative thinking of several craftsmen. Many of these announcements set forth the newest ideas of our most inventive scientists. By reading about their triumphs we tend to spur our own creative spirit.

5.

Too many of us let our minds serve solely as sponges while reading. Instead of such passivity, Elliott Dunlap Smith of Yale has urged active effort—enough energy to "*exercise* our power of creative thought."

George Bernard Shaw went so far as to write his own outline of each book he was about to read before he even opened it. After finishing the volume he would compare his own version with that of the author—and would usually decide that G.B.S. had won.

During the long, long trial of Communist leaders, Judge Harold R. Medina devoted his week ends to reading. As to how he reads, here's what Jack Alexander reported: "He would read Dickens for a while. Characteristically, this adventure was thorough and methodical. He started it off by reading a biography of Dickens. On reaching a mention of one of the novels, he would set the biography aside long enough to read the novel, then return to the biography until another novel was mentioned."

In *How to Read a Book*, Mortimer Adler distinguishes between *information* and *enlightenment* as results of reading—a distinction that determines the extent to which reading can foster creative imagination. To gain enlightenment we must think as we read. Thus more ideas "come to us" from reading. Often they are sparked by passages wholly unrelated to the creative thought we generate.

According to Adler, the art of reading "includes all the same skills that are involved in the art of discovery; keenness of observation, readily available memory, range of imagination, and, of course, a reason trained in analysis and reflection."

In Fritz Kunkel's book on the implications of the Gospel

according to Saint Matthew, Kunkel holds that there are two ways of reading the Bible or any other book—the "static" way, and the "dynamic" way. The dynamic way calls for putting ourselves into what we read, and thus exercising imagination.

Reading provides far better creative exercise when we make notes as we go. For one thing, this induces more energy on our part. In Albert Bigelow Paine's life of Mark Twain the biographer wrote: "On the table by him, and on his bed, and on the billiard-room shelves, he kept the books he read most. All, or nearly all, had annotations—spontaneously uttered marginal notes, title prefatories, or concluding comments. They were the books he had read again and again, and it was seldom that he had not had something to say with each fresh reading."

Every book provides plenty of blank flyleaves on which we can do as Bruce Barton does. What's that? Simply this— when we come to a stirring passage, we can stop and make a note of its gist and the number of the page. Thus we can create an index of our own.

Then, too, if we go at it right, we will think up many ideas of our own as we read. It is quite as important for us to record these brain-children of ours as to list the author's gems.

6.

Ministers' sons represent far less than one per cent of our population, and yet, in Who's Who in America, nearly 10 per cent of those listed were sons of clergymen. England has far more lawyers than clergymen; and yet, in England's Who's Who, sons of clergymen outnumber sons of lawyers two to one; and they outnumber doctors' sons by three to one.

Similar ratios held true among our great men of the past. Ministers' sons included statesmen like Wilson, Hughes, Cleveland, Clay, Buchanan and Arthur; financiers like Harriman and Cecil Rhodes; scientists like Agassiz, Jenner, Linnaeus, and Morse of Atlantic Cable fame; artists like Reynolds; architects like Sir Christopher Wren; authors like Tennyson, Ben Jonson, Cowper, Goldsmith, Coleridge, Addison, Matthew Arnold and Emerson.

The record of clergymen's sons reflects their knowledge and their higher ability to think. Then, too, the fact that pastors are usually hard put financially may tend to invest their sons with greater drive. Moreover, many of these boys came from non-urban areas, where they filled their creative fuel tanks with firsthand experiences in their youths.

But over and above all that is the fact that—more so than in other family circles—children brought up in pastoral homes are exposed to good literature. They early acquire a lifelong habit of the right kind of reading.

To create a new sermon each week, a minister has to dig hard—he has to mine ideas out of his reading or risk losing his flock. Thus he sets an example for his sons. The fact that so many of them grow up to excel in creative ability is evidence of the way we can train imagination by reading *what* we should, the *way* we should.

7.

But of course we can read too much—just as we can drink too much water, or bask too long in the sunshine. According to Alfred North Whitehead, "Great readers who exclude other activities are not distinguished by subtlety of brain. They tend to be timid conventional thinkers. No doubt this is partly due to their excessive knowledge outrunning their powers of thought; but it is partly due to the lack of brain-stimulus from the productive activities of hand or voice."

Especially when we are on a long creative quest, such as a research project, we can suffocate our own ideas with over-reading. Schopenhauer warned against this danger, and so did Graham Wallas. Kettering continually urged his creative associates to spend more time in trying to think up hypotheses than in sopping up too many facts from books—especially from textbooks.

By and large, however, reading is most helpful to imagination, and mainly because, through reading, we can store up food for creative thinking. Hughes Mearns summed this up: "The right sort of reading is rich in vitamins. Those who have been deprived of its energizing units may suffer later dangers in abbreviated lives. We must in honesty admit, however, that many are able to thrive upon its near substitute, a rich reading of experience; but that requires a much longer process."

All of which adds up to the fact that, if we invest our reading with imaginative effort, and if we select what to read on the basis of its creative nourishment, we can do much to build up the most precious of our mental gifts.

Chapter 8

SEDENTARY GAMES can

bring imagination into play

E ARNEST ELMO CALKINS compiled a list of 250 different kinds of sedentary games. On analysis, only about 50 of these entail creative effort. Luckily, the ones that exercise our minds are the best fun.

Much depends on how we play. In chess, for instance, we can either be "book players," and make all moves from memory—or we can make each move a creative adventure, as does a scientist who is one of the best chess players I know. "Instead of playing chess by rote," he told me, "I continually try to think up new and dashing ways to gain my goals. This makes the game more fun and better mental exercise."

Mark Twain applied an impish imagination to his billiard-playing by continually thinking up new and ludicrous ways to play that staid old game. We don't have to go berserk to derive creative exercise from such pastimes, but a lot does depend on how imaginatively we go at them.

2.

Does puzzle-solving do more than amuse? Thomas Edison's answer to that question would be a decided *yes*. According to his son Charles, his father definitely believed in this pastime as creative exercise.

More people do crosswords than any other kind of puzzle; and yet surprisingly few even look at them. Readership surveys of newspapers show that only six per cent of their readers ever glance at the crossword feature; whereas 90 per cent scan the picture page. Most women look at obituaries (twice as many women as men). The comics get a big play from both sexes and all ages. Almost at the bottom of the list of features come the crosswords.

We can combine creative practice with relaxation by solving such puzzles, especially examples as tough as those in the Sunday edition of the *New York Times*. To unriddle them, we must work our minds backward and forward. But mainly, we must *work* our minds; and that, of itself, tones up our creative fiber.

What's another way of saying "stared down"? In the first place, is it active? Or is it passive? Is it in the past tense? Was, or is, someone doing the staring? Or is someone, or something, being stared at?

We know that there are seven letters in the word, or words. We cast our minds hither and thither. We think of "ogle"; but that doesn't fit. We try to visualize a person in the act of staring down. We begin to feel that the answer is not in our own vocabulary and that therefore there is nothing in our memories which we can dig up by way of the answer.

We send our minds down one blind alley after another, and then again we try to visualize a person in the act of staring. Ah, the *eyes!* Of course that must be the key. From that we try to build a word around eye—a word entirely new to us. You have probably arrived at the answer long before this—*out-eyed.*

What's a five-letter word for California? It can't be *sunny,* because the fourth letter is S. You whip your mind hither and thither—now in search of Spanish roots—then in search of slang along the line of "Frisco." You keep on beating your brains. And finally, with an absurd degree of satisfaction, you hit upon the answer—*Coast.* In winning that tussle with the puzzler you have well exercised your imaginative muscles.

For more strenuous creative training, try the Double Crostics, which a woman, Elizabeth Kingsley, originated and exclusively produced. She told me this: "Mere knowledge alone cannot solve my Double Crostics. I construct them so that they require creative thinking above all else." Double Crostic fans have included many of our most creative notables—Kenneth Roberts, Christopher Morley, Elmer Rice, and Rupert Hughes, to mention only four. A publisher remarked, "When you solve one of Mrs. Kingsley's puzzles, every millimeter of your gray matter is glowing—the way a gymnast's muscles glow after a workout."

In doing crosswords and Double Crostics, even if we have known the word we seek, the act of bringing it out of our memory induces mental effort. If the wanted word is beyond our ken, the act of trying to guess what it is entails a creative process. We must synthesize certain clues to sleuth out the answer. Out of the thin air, we must pick one alternative after another until we hit upon the right one.

We benefit also because such efforts tend to improve our vocabulary. According to human engineers, the number of words we know is a significant measure of our leadership ability. Tests have proved that those in high places uniformly excel in their knowledge of words. Whether this be the cause of their success, or merely a coincidental result of their experience on the way up, is an open question.

"Is it cheating when you look it up in the dictionary?" a little boy asked me while I was doing a crossword puzzle; and that brings up a question. Do such puzzles do us more good when we try to solve them without benefit of reference books? I think so. Although we can gain a wider knowledge by looking up this and that, by thus leaning on reference books we tend to take the edge off the creative exercise which puzzles can provide.

Elizabeth Kingsley, for one, would probably challenge

that contention. I once told her that, on a train between New York and Wilmington, I had completely worked out one of her Double Crostics without benefit of books. Her sweet reply indicated that she felt she had fallen down in creating a puzzle as easy to solve as all that.

As a most strenuous creative exercise, just try to create a crossword puzzle on your own. Having concocted a few myself, I can testify that to make up a really good one calls for more creative power than I have as yet achieved. Every year brings more and more new kinds of crossword puzzles, and more ways of presenting them. Just try thinking up still another new way, if you don't mind taxing your imagination to the limit.

To give your creative mind an even more strenuous workout, try creating and deciphering codes. As a pastime, this dark science of secret communication is as old as Egypt. Civilians who make a hobby of cryptograms not only exercise their creativity to the limit, but also train themselves for heroic service in our nation's defense. When war comes, these volunteers are given life-and-death responsibilities almost overnight.

Organizations of such cryptographers have sprung up all over America. In Boston, they are called "Yankee Puzzlers"; in Rochester, "Genesee Owls"; in Fall River, "Bed Warmers." Of about 20 of these groups, the largest is the New York Cryptographers Society, most of whose members are graduates of the course which Hunter College gives in this brainracking hobby. Last year, over 800 people signed up for those classes, but only 25 finished—a fact that may prove this creative exercise to be too drastic for most of us humans to undertake.

3.

Well, let's relax a minute and talk about something easier, like card-playing. A friend of mine called this pastime "the last resort of feeble minds." Although he smiled when he said that, he seriously charges that in playing card games, we are tempted to take the attitude "What's the use of trying? It's all in the deal." He also holds that the rules are so rigid that they clip the creative wings of the players.

Although card-playing does offer too little creative exercise, plenty of ingenuity has been put into thinking up more and more kinds of games. The varieties of poker are endless. There are 41 different kinds of rummy, including Canasta. Vernon Quinn devised 50 card games especially for children. There are over 100 brands of solitaire. These serve well as time-killers, but that's about all that can be said for them.

Rummy provides a wishy-washy workout. As I write this, I hold in my hand the score sheet of a series of gin games I played with a friend of mine one Saturday afternoon at our golf club when the rain kept us off the course. This record shows that he won 48 times, and I won six times. I feel sure that the cards had quite a lot to do with my débâcle. While he was shuffling for his 20th victory, my mind wandered to the question of creative exercise, and I thought to myself: "The only way I can use my imagination during this ordeal is to think of the many other ways in which I am lucky." Thus I kept myself from bemoaning the way the cards were running against me.

Although many of my friends play Canasta, I regard this mainly as a test of the aptitude which human engineers call "finger dexterity." True, it does make us push our brain cells around a shade more actively than does rummy—but far too gently—and far too rigidly, in line with the rules.

Some hold that poker is an imaginative pastime. John McDonald has called it "a contest of strategies." And he adds: "The mark of good poker-playing is deception." To fool one's cronies in a game in which they are equally versed undoubtedly does call imagination into play to some degree. But that is only a slight factor, compared to the run of the cards and the use of judgment.

Contract bridge is probably a better wit-sharpener. But mainly it calls for analytical judgment plus a knowledge of proved techniques. Miles Robertson, President of Oneida Community, has awed me with his ability to see through the hands of the other three players—almost as if their cards were made of glass. Such magic does entail some imagination.

Another man I play with is Duncan MacLeod, likewise a manufacturer. He shows his power of imagination by his uncanny ability to foresee all tricks. His friends josh him about his habit of throwing his cards face-up on the table—before they are played out—and then announcing: "We are down two" . . . or . . . "We have all the rest" . . . or whatever the result might be. Strangers sometimes challenge him; but when they review the hands they find the outcome to be exactly as Dunc had foreseen after only a few of the tricks had been played.

The sad fact is that imaginative playing is usually at a penalty, even in bridge. We risk undermining our partner's skill when we depart from the conventions in the slightest degree. When we think up radical tactics, we tend to mislead him—and thus tend to lead our team to downfall.

4.

Of the 35 parlor pastimes which provide entertainment and mental exercise for small groups, the best known is "20 Questions." This game forces the questioners to push their minds around in search of alternatives; and to that extent it exercises *their* creativity. The others, however, are called upon for almost no mental effort.

A brain-stretcher based on verbiage is called "Inky Pinky." In this, you have to think up a rhymed equivalent for a simple statement. For example, an answer to "five-cent cucumber" could be "nickel pickle." This game can be so simple as to become insipid; or it can be stretched in ways that strain our imaginative muscles. One way to toughen it is by limiting answers to words of not less than three syllables. Thus, "a Communist descended from an ape" becomes an "evolutionary revolutionary."

At lunch with four of our young writers, I marveled at the way they inky-pinkied each other. One of them asked, "Could you give me a dark hint?" Another quickly replied, "You mean a clandestine suggestion?" The third came back with "How about a drunken Indian?" The answer turned out to be a "hiccupy Chicopee." Later they outlawed rhyming words of less than four syllables. Thus, "a panic on a plane" became "a Constellation consternation" and "a profitable bedding plant" became a "satisfactory mattress-factory."

All that may sound a bit childish; but creative people take to this pastime and believe that it does something to sharpen their creative wits. One group that frequently plays this game includes a psychiatrist, a radio announcer, an artist and an editor. In our Cleveland office, our creative people frequently have to travel by car to Canton and Akron. En route back home they nearly always play Inky Pinky. Thus they shorten the trip and hone their thinking tools.

Another game along the same line was introduced in June 1950 by *Vogue* and is called "Cliché." The editors announced it as "a handy pastime requiring no equipment other than a few old chestnuts, an occasional red herring, and a free-wheeling imagination." This is a game where puns are at a premium. You think of a worn-out expression and then, without disclosing that theme, you illustrate it with a far-fetched anecdote of your own invention. The others then have to guess what title by way of a cliché would best fit your yarn.

Vogue outlined 10 techniques which you can employ in this game. Here's an example of the "embroidery" method: "A scientist conducting I.Q. tests among animals found a young deer that was most cooperative and did very well indeed. Then one day an imported alcoholic beverage of high proof was added to the deer's drinking water by a prankish bystander—with rather interesting results. After several swigs, the deer, in its impassioned desire to be even more cooperative, almost overwhelmed the scientist with solicitous affection."

Of course you have already worked out the answer to that; and you may not like it. What is it? "Absinthe makes the hart grow fonder."

5.

Healthful creative exercise can be had from parlor games based on acting things out. If bluffing at poker calls for an ounce of imagination, pantomime calls for pounds.

Unlike "20 Questions," which activates no one except the questioner, charades not only challenge the ingenuity of those who enact them, but also stimulate the viewers to try hard to imagine the meaning of each gesture and facial expression. This is especially true of the improved version of charades now called "The Game."

A still newer version might well be called "Picturades." In this, the visualization is done by drawing, instead of by acting. A master of ceremonies writes down a short list of titles or sayings. The rest of the group is divided into teams of three or four players. The master of ceremonies secretly communicates the first phrase to one member in each group. This person then goes to work with pad and pencil and draws pictures designed to enable his teammates quickly to guess the given phrase. The team which first comes up with the right answer wins that inning.

Amateur theatricals supply good creative exercise to those who do the acting and to those who put on the production. In a Junior League Show last winter I saw some amazing acts which had been created by people who had never known that they could create. Young mothers composed the music as well as wrote the words for topical songs that were almost worthy of Broadway. A daughter of mine had charge of the props; and what ingenuity she used in order to make a dime do the work of a dollar!

Our family spent a Thanksgiving with the Frank Hatches near Boston. On our arrival there that afternoon, after a decent interval of politeness, our host told us that we would have to sing—or do something—for our dinner. He announced that, in that living room at five o'clock, a vaudeville show would start, and that each of us would meanwhile have to write an act which we, ourselves, would have to put on.

He was kind enough to prime our pumps, however. To my wife and oldest daughter he assigned "a skit in a five-and-ten store." He signed up my son for "a burlesque on a college cheer-leader." As my topic he handed me: "Martin, Barton and Fish."

Then, singly or by teams, we all went to work to prepare our acts. Did I say "work"? Every one of us had more fun than a barrel of kittens. And when the show went on, we waxed uproarious—we split our sides as we watched each other stumble through his or her freshly created and unrehearsed production.

The male Hatches, father and son, climaxed the show with a series of newly born songs about us guests, with the two of them doing the singing and the piano-playing in duet. I would like to say that their music as well as their words were original; but of course the ditties had to be parodies. Lest Frank take umbrage at this disclosure, I will whisper to the reader that he *has* composed the music of several popular songs—a pastime which is but one of about a dozen of his creative hobbies.

6.

Such games as dominoes and backgammon bring imagination into play—but not to the extent that chess and checkers do. As between these latter two games—if it hadn't been for George Wales I might be advising my readers: "If you're going to play checkers, play chess instead. Chess is a better creative exercise."

George Wales is a friend of mine who built a fortune out of his mechanical inventions. As one of his "handcraft" hobbies, he handles his own earth-moving, bricklaying, and carpentry on his 150-acre estate. His chief avocation is checkers. Solely to house this hobby he rents the entire 22nd floor of an office building. He there employs a full-time staff which has amassed the world's largest checker library, valued at $250,000.

One of his researchers does nothing but clip articles from foreign newspapers of the last two centuries. For example, here is a historic bit that she dug up from a newspaper published in Newcastle, England, on October 11, 1873: "The British Museum exhibits a checkerboard invented in Egypt and said to be 6000 years old. Whist was invented for the amusement of an insane king; chess and draughts (checkers) are known to exercise a beneficial effect in certain cases of dementia."

George Wales maintains that nothing can exercise our creative muscles the way checkers can. He recently told me: "With all of my practice as an inventor, I find that checkers can call for more imagination than any machine I ever created. There are so many possible moves in checkers that if every human being in the world were to make one move every five minutes, it would take a thousand years to make them all."

Wales holds that Edgar Allan Poe best summarized the superiority of checkers over chess. "In chess, where the pieces have different and bizarre motions, what is complex is taken for what is profound. In checkers, any advantage gained by either party is gained by superior acumen."

George Wales divides his time between his checker office and his factory, where he produces the machines he originated. He claims that the effort he devotes to creating and solving checker problems makes him a more prolific inventor.

Paradoxically, he admits that his checker-playing is the hardest kind of mental labor, and yet he finds that it relaxes him—enables him to tackle his factory problems with a fresher mind.

Wales owns patents on about 25 checker-playing devices. One of these is called "Train the Brain." The checkers are magnetized and the board is of metal. It is about as high and wide as this book. The back of the board accommodates movable cards, each showing a "puzzler"—a set-up such as would come toward the end of a game. First you move the reds, then the blacks, in an effort to beat the blacks. Unlike solitaire, you can play this lying down. And, unlike solitaire, your success depends not on a lucky shuffle but on your ingenuity. But Mr. Wales is kindly. If you finally have to give up, you can find the winning series of moves on the back of the card.

George Wales' contagion got me. For the first time since I grew up I tried this ancient game once again, but made the mistake of taking on a teen-ager who could really play. I finally got a draw in our third contest. "Want to play another?" he asked. "No, thanks," I replied. "I have to get back to work." What I did was to return to my labors on this book you are now reading. I had not told the lad the whole truth—those three games had tired my mind to a point where I sought literary effort as a relief.

Chess or checkers—either can be good practice, if we go at them wholeheartedly. If we play at them unimaginatively, we might almost as well twiddle our thumbs—a truth which applies equally to every kind of pastime.

Chapter 9

INDOOR SPORTS as sources

of creative exercise

SO MUCH FOR sit-down games. Now let's look over the pastimes which bring our bodies into play; and let's see to what extent these games and sports call for imagination.

The first great invention of man was the wheel. Close cousin to that is the ball, around which most of our sports have been devised.

"Games played with a ball stamp no character on the mind," according to Thomas Jefferson. As opposed to that, we have the saying, attributed to Lord Wellington, that the battle of Waterloo was won "on the playing fields of Eton."

As mind-developers, most of such games fall short because they call for too much speed to permit of deliberate cerebration. This point is illustrated by the story Mac Davis tells about Yogi Berra, hard-hitting catcher of the Yankees:

Yogi was swinging at the first pitch, whether high or low or wide. His manager bellowed at him: "Try to *think* before you cut at the ball." On his next time up, Yogi watched three perfect pitches sail by him, and the umpire yelled, "You're out!" Back in the dugout, Yogi mumbled: "I don't get it. How can a guy think and hit at the same time?"

Yogi was right. In a series of scientific demonstrations, William W. Harper has proved how much time it takes to cerebrate. He was called in on a case where a driver claimed that he had applied his brakes within "a thousandth of a second" after first seeing the pedestrian whom he had run over and killed. In court, Harper brought forth a piece of pipe eight inches long; he asked the opposing lawyer to put his hand flat against the bottom, and to withdraw it as fast as he could. Harper then dropped a marble through the hole, and it hit the lawyer's hand before he could pull it away. Since this fall took one-fifth of a second it proved that no mind could think fast enough to put on brakes within anything like "one-thousandth of a second."

Since our speediest reflexes are as slow as that, it is obvious that in fast-moving contests we can count only on instinct. There just isn't time for creative thinking in the heat of battle.

2.

Which offers better mental exercise—billiards or pool? I say billiards, by all means. During many a winter I wasted my Saturday afternoons driving balls into pockets. Recently, I took up billiards. I find that both games yield physical exercise by way of walking, but that billiards calls for far more creative thinking than does pool.

The simplest form is "straight-rail," in which you try to make your cue ball hit first one and then the other ball, no matter how. Even that calls for imaginative effort. But "three-cushion" billiards? *Wow!* In this you have to make your cue ball hit at least three side-rails in the course of hitting the two other balls. Sometimes you cannot make your point without hitting four or five cushions en route. To visualize each shot in advance, you must use imagination akin to that which an architect puts into dreaming up a new building.

The proficiency of older men at billiards is another proof that, although age may fade other faculties, it need not shrivel imagination—at least not the kind of visual thinking-ahead that billiards calls for. Two of the most skillful billiard players I knew were Henry Boller, age 92, and General Louis Babcock, age 82.

Mark Twain kept up his billiards until shortly before he died at the age of 75. He often spent as much as nine hours a day at his table. His favorite opponent was Albert Bigelow Paine, who later wrote: "He followed the endless track around the table with the light step of youth. At three or four in the morning he would urge one more game and would taunt me for my weariness." Here is how Paine spent Twain's 71st birthday with him: "We played billiards all day. He invented a new game for the occasion, originating new rules at almost every shot."

Judge Medina recently went at billiards with characteristic zeal. He chose the game because of its mental challenge. He installed a table in his home, took lessons, practices continually, and keeps copious notes of what he learns from week to week. He hopes that after five years of such study and practice he will be able to play well.

The game of billiards is recommended. As a relaxation, it refreshes our minds. As a mental exercise, it calls upon imagination for every shot.

3.

Now let's look at some sports in which only a few indulge but which many watch. Wrestling, for instance, may be worth a mention because of its spectacular rise in popularity—due mainly to the many new ideas that have been thought up by promoters, and by wrestlers and their managers.

Never since the gladiators made Rome ring with cheers from the Colisseum has so much color been put into any sport —color by way of lurid costumes, and color by way of outlandish dramatics.

Gorgeous George became a wrestling champion in the anomalous guise of a dandy, with his gentleman's gentleman spraying the ring with disinfectant and spraying him with perfume. He dresses in the finery of a Cleopatra. Of his 90 robes, all designed by himself, one is caped with genuine ermine.

Chief Don Eagle puts on an act in honor of his Indian ancestry. His father serves as his second. Both wear tribal feathers as they enter the ring.

Crowds that dislike aristocracy pack the arenas to see Lord Blears, accompanied by his manager, a British captain with a monocle. Another favorite is a commoner, Don Marlin, who appears barefoot, clad in frayed trousers, carrying his suckling pig, Clementine. The fans cheer when he nurses Clementine out of a bottle.

New and surprising ideas have been put into the antics as well as into the accessories. Almost every mayhem expert has a lethal trick, supposedly of his own invention. Farmer Marlin's "Mule Kick" is a roof raiser. The throngs never tire of the endless variations on the noble technique of lifting one's opponent into the air, landing him on top of the ropes, and then tangling his legs hopelessly between the strands.

Best-liked of all are the "accidents" which force the referee into the act—"unintentional" antics such as leap-frogging over his shoulders in order to land head first into the stomach of one's opponent, or falling on the referee, and pinning him down by "mistake."

Wrestling is not recommended as a creative exercise. But, regardless of how we esteem or condemn the sport, we must admit that its box-office success is a tribute to the power of new ideas.

4.

Boxing has been in the doldrums, partly because, since the Marquess of Queensberry's time, no new ideas have enlivened this sport.

The boxers themselves must move too fast to think creatively during their bouts. But they can do with imagination in conceiving their plans of battle. Two of our greatest champions were not "naturals"—Jim Corbett and Gene Tunney. Each went to the top by using his head.

Corbett dethroned John L. Sullivan by means of a boxing stratagem he had thought up. "It was entirely new for that day," he reported in his autobiography. He feared what might happen if he were cornered by the savage Sullivan. "So," he said, "I made up my mind to let him corner me while I was still fresh. Then I could find out what he would try to do when he got me there."

During the first two rounds, Jim let the champ back him into corner after corner. Then, in the third round, when cornered once again, "I loosed a left hand for his face with all the power I had." That was exactly as Jim had planned. It spelled the end of the great John L., who worshipped brawn and scoffed at brains.

Some pugilists do put imagination into their generalship; but we spectators who enjoy watching a prizefight, either on television or at the arena, might just as well watch cats on our backyard fence for all the creative exercise that pugilism affords us.

5.

Sports announcers tell me that the toughest game to broadcast is hockey, because of its breakneck speed, which likewise makes creative cerebration all but impossible for the players.

Creative thinking goes with hockey, as it does with boxing, mainly in master-minding. The ex-players who serve as managers usually sink or rise according to their ability to think up maneuvers.

During the game, however, a contestant may sometimes bring his imagination into play, as did King Clancy in the story reported by Tony Wurzer. Eddie Shore and his Boston Bruins were five goals ahead of Toronto. Clancy figured that his Maple Leafs could win if they could get Shore off the ice. When he drew a minor penalty and started toward the penalty box, Clancy grabbed him and yelled:

"You gonna let that bum get away with a raw decision like that? I saw it all, sure, and that referee is blind. Even if you're on the opposition, I can't stand this unfairness. I can't."

Shore bit. He savagely whipped the puck at the referee, and drew a 10-minute misconduct penalty. By the time he got back, the Leafs had scored enough goals to win.

An associate of mine, Tax Cumings, played goalie for Harvard a generation ago. He was then highly creative, and has kept growing more so ever since. Part of his success in keeping enemy pucks out of Harvard's net was due to his ideas. One of his new wrinkles had to do with his equipment.

When a puck bangs against a goalie's shinguards, it often rebounds to where an opposing player can slash it into the net. "How can I keep the puck from bouncing back?" That was the problem Cumings gave himself. He finally devised a plan by which he attached wet sponges to the front of his shinguards, and they did the trick. It was not until years later that other goalies caught on to this goal-saving gadget.

Hockey provides us spectators with relaxation and also quickens our spirit. On leaving a Canadian arena after watching a hard-fought game, I usually feel a step-up in my sense of drive. Such a surge of effort is good for creativity. But only in this minor way does hockey qualify as a developer of imagination for us who merely look on.

6.

As for other indoor sports, the one that calls for utmost speed of mind and body is fencing. Here, too, the action is too fast to allow for any real thinking. To a slightly lesser degree, this is also true of handball, badminton, squash and tennis.

Bowling abounds in sociability and provides healthful recreation. Its popularity has grown so great that, according to recent estimates, there are now over 25,000,000 Americans who bowl regularly each season. The game ranks low as creative exercise, not because it is too fast for cogitation, but because its technique narrows down almost solely to hitting the right pin in the right spot.

Basketball embraces far more people, both as players and as spectators, than most of us realize. As for the participants, here again the sport is so fast that instinct must take the place of cerebration. The coaches and the captains, however, have to think out the tactics in advance; to them the game is therefore a real creative challenge. The good to the spectators is about the same as in hockey-watching.

*   *   *

All in all, indoor sports do but little to develop creativity. Personally, I like them; and I don't consider them as entirely wasteful of my time because, in between spurts of creative effort, I need such relaxation in order to let incubation get in its licks—as explained in a later chapter.

Chapter 10

OUTDOOR SPORTS— can they

provide creative exercise?

O UTDOOR SPORTS TEND to bring our minds more or less into play, depending upon how creatively we go at them. This is illustrated by that beloved and accursed game called golf.

"The less you think, the better you play." Several pros have so advised me. For them, and for others who may have absorbed a natural swing early in life, thinklessness and effortlessness are undoubtedly indicated. But as for us hackers who started when our hair began to grey—we would dub even worse than we do if we did not "think" our way through every shot from address to finish. Such "thinking," however, is non-creative—it merely puts memory to a speed test.

The place for imaginative effort is not on the course but on the practice tee. Here you can get more bodily exercise in far less time, and you can get creative exercise as well.

All my friends berate me because I practice far more than I play. My defense is that my practice is mainly experimentation. Unlike Judge Medina, who repeats the same swing for hours at a time, I try a new and different form on almost every shot—always hoping that it may lead to the discovery of a simpler, surer way to play golf.

Of late, my scientific son-in-law has discouraged me by pointing out the almost infinite number of changes that can be made in stance, grip, tempo, sequence and all that. He estimates that these permutations and combinations permit of about 10 million different swings. I fear I may not live long enough to cry "Eureka!"

My pseudo knowledge has irritated many a great golfer. I believe myself to be the only pupil ever fired by a pro for insubordination. During a lesson, the famous Ernie Jones growled at me for the 15th time: "I told you to *swing* it."

"Which way?" I asked.

"There is only *one* way to *swing*," he retorted.

"Okay, Mr. Jones," I peeved, "you just watch while I show you 57 different ways of swinging a club."

But he would have none of my demonstration. With dignity and determination he announced: "Your lesson is over. And I never want to see you again."

Creative thinking in personal relations can help make golf more fun. As a result of some luck I found myself opposed to the club champion for that year's title. I knew he would beat me. It was only a question of how soon.

I played better than I knew how; so it was not until the 15th hole that George Weimert finished me off. After sinking his putt for that birdie, he expected me to shake his hand; but, instead, I handed him a sealed envelope. He opened it, and read this letter—addressed to him and signed by me:

"You are a worthy champion. I was just plain lucky to get into the semi-finals against you. I would rather be put out by you than anybody I can think of. Hearty congratulations!"

Another use for imagination is to think up gentle ways to offset discourtesy, as when a friend of mine found himself matched against a golfer who unnerved opponents by standing endlessly over his ball before hitting. For that match, my friend took along a book which he opened and read each time his opponent began to get ready to prepare to condition himself to start swinging.

We derive walking exercise, but no thinking exercise, from watching golf. A slight exception is when the gallery is huge, as at the Masters' Tournament. Then the spectators stretch their ingenuity to the limit trying to think up how to get as near as they can to their favorite player without being beaned by his backswing.

2.

Gus H. Baseballfan mainly pays to see his favorite player lift the sphere over the fence with the bases loaded. Most spectators resemble the girl who joined her date late at the ball park. The scoreboard showed that both teams were scoreless at the end of the eighth. She exclaimed: "Oh goody! We haven't missed *anything!*"

Although baseball offers little or no creative exercise to spectators, it does call for creative thinking by the players. Unlike other sports in which the action is almost continuous, ball games are mainly made up of intervals between innings, between batters, between pitches. These lulls allow time for conscious thinking ahead.

And the problem continually changes with variable factors, such as: who's at bat, who's on base and where, what inning it is, what the score is, how many are out, and what the count is on the batter. In addition to the versatile thinking each of these situations calls for, baseball continually challenges its players to bat up something different by way of new ideas.

Creative imagination on the part of the batter often pays off. In a Cleveland-Detroit game, Hal Newhauser handcuffed Cleveland's Al Rosen with inside pitches his first three times at bat. Rosen came up again with men on base. Hal's first two pitches cut the inside corner. Then, just as Newhauser hurled the third, Rosen took one full step back and belted the ball for a double. He had foreseen that another inside pitch was coming and had figured how to meet it solidly.

Before each toss, a pitcher has to think of a score of alternatives. "How about that runner? . . . Can I pick him off

with that lead or should I just leisurely chase him back?"
. . . "What if this batter bunts?" . . . "If the ball comes my
way, shall I throw it to second or to first?" . . . "Shall I pitch
that floater the catcher's calling for, or should I shake off
his sign?" All that, and more, calls for thinking ahead, as well
as for choosing the right alternative.

Infielders likewise have to foresee a dozen contingencies.
And the outfielders? They just catch the ball on the fly or on
the bounce, and then throw it in on the run? Ty Cobb was
not content with that routine. Several times each season, the
runner on second would be lured into a sense of false security
through being ignored by the second baseman and the shortstop. Suddenly the pitcher would snap the throw to Ty Cobb,
who had sneaked in from the outfield to cover second. And
the fans were treated to the unusual spectacle of a runner
being tagged out in the infield by an outfielder.

The catcher must use his imagination the most. He has to
think up an endless list of alternatives before he squats. The
over-all team strategy revolves around him. In addition, he
receives and relays most of the signals from the bench. A
smart catcher gives the manager the equivalent of a playing
coach in the field—and he is treasured above rubies.

The creative training a catcher receives usually pays off in
later life, as evidenced by the long list of catchers who have
stood out as big-league managers. One Cornelius McGilli-
cuddy—the beloved "Connie Mack" of the Athletics—deserves
first mention. Others include John "Muggsy" McGraw, Ray
Schalk, Frank Leroy Chance, Roger Bresnahan, Bill Kelleher,
Fred Mitchell, Mickey Cochrane, Steve O'Neill and Paul
Richards.

Richards became the outstanding baseball manager of
1951 by pulling his Sox up from the cellar. "What makes
Richards great?" asked sports writer Cy Kritzer. And he
answered: "Richards has the daring imagination to throw the
book away when circumstances invite it. He has no regard
for tradition that says you can't move a pitcher over to play

third base while you bring in a lefthander to pitch to one batter. He won his laurels as a World Series catcher mainly through his resourcefulness. His never-tiring efforts to think up new and better tactics are the main secret of his managerial success."

Ray Schalk was another heady catcher I observed first-hand. In the old days, when a throw to first went wild, the runner always kept going. Schalk thought up how to stop that. As soon as the ball was hit fair, he actually raced the runner to first base. All catchers have since adopted that tactic. Luke Easter was an early victim of this plan. He was running to first. The throw went wild. He took two steps toward second, only to discover that the catcher had backed up the play and had him cold.

Ball players are continually challenged to think up new wrinkles. Bob Feller's pick-off play at second base in a recent World Series was so smart and so smooth that even the umpire missed it—as movies of the play proved afterward. Lou Boudreau, according to Taylor Spink of *The Sporting News*, originated the anti-Williams shift on July 14, 1946, at Boston. Ted Williams had been hitting hard and often—always to the right. When he next came to bat, Lou Boudreau packed all Cleveland infielders between second and first, moved his center fielder into right field, and posted his left fielder behind shortstop. This strategy stopped Williams.

Some new wrinkles are not quite cricket. One such was the antic thought up by Eddie Stanky. Playing second, he was directly in line with the batter's vision; so he just jumped up and down and waved his arms while the pitcher threw. There was no rule against this defensive tactic. It worked such havoc that Commissioner Happy Chandler finally asked Stanky to cease and desist.

Much of the modern equipment was originated not by manufacturers, but by players. Roger Bresnahan introduced shinguards for catchers in 1907. Fred Thayer originated the mask in 1875.

And the psychological quirks that have been thought up by players! Ernie Bonham carried an iron sphere, so that the baseball would feel lighter when he pitched. Ty Cobb initiated the custom of swinging three bats before going to the plate, thus making his own warclub seem like a toothpick. And he practiced with weights in his shoes to strengthen his legs.

All in all, the "ivory" of baseball players could well be emulated by the hordes of us who merely watch and creatively go to seed in the ball park.

3.

In high school I played football fiendishly. But at college, I weighed only 120; so the best I could do was to become varsity manager. My love for the game has kept me actively interested ever since.

As an ardent spectator I have used my imagination to anticipate each play. My usual companions have been boys, including my son. And how I would show off for them! Whenever I guessed the next play right, I preened myself a-plenty.

When my son and his friends were about 10 we went to a crucial game. All through the first half, I vocally masterminded the home team from my seat of vantage high up in the grandstand. Then, early in the second half, when I predicted a quick kick, a young man in front of us looked around and politely said, "No, this is going to be a forward pass." He turned out to be right; and my six juvenile guests enjoyed my humiliation. This indignity went on and on. Each time I would prophesy, he would turn around and correct me with devastating accuracy.

When the game ended, I put my hand on his shoulder and asked, "Are you one of the coaching staff?" "No," he replied, "but I quarterbacked Purdue last year, and we played exactly the same system." My boy companions are now married men; but they still look back and laugh at my red face.

Gridiron players use the same kind of catch-as-catch-can thinking as do boxers, wrestlers or tennis players. Since soccer is not run on signals, each player is even more on his own than in football.

Alan Ward, Jr., plays in the line, and he claims that even linesmen must use vicarious imagination: "I plan to meet the other guy where I figure *I'd* come through if I were in his shoes. If I'm wrong too much of the time, I'll spend the season on the bench."

The quarterback must call upon his creative imagination every minute his team is on the offensive. His reasoning may be largely intuitive; but, even while walking back to his huddle, a good quarterback must apply hard creative thinking as to what play to call for next.

This fact is recognized by sports writers. Often you see quarterbacks described the way Ray Ryan described Don Holland: "His play-calling was daring and imaginative."

In pro football, however, a quarterback is likely to find his coach doing much of his creative thinking for him. For instance, Paul Brown, mentor of the world champions, was known to call 90 per cent of Cleveland's plays. After almost every scrimmage he sent in a new guard with instructions for the quarterback.

Football coaches reach creative heights, not only in planning basic strategies and in calling individual plays, but in the way they set their teams on fire. Of the many stories which illustrate this point I like best the one about Knute Rockne. Notre Dame was waging its annual battle against the Army, and getting pushed all over the field. At half time, the Irish braced themselves in the locker room for Rockne's tirade. Five, ten, fifteen minutes went by, but no Rockne. Then, with two minutes to go, the Rock stuck his head in the door, looked at his players with a wry smile and said, "Let's go, *girls*." Notre Dame won the game in the second half.

So many coaches have risen to heights of mental achievement in later life that I venture the opinion that the time they spent in coaching proved to be a post-graduate course in creative thinking. Rockne was one example. Herman Hickman of Yale is another. And then I always think of Harold Tenney. He played for Princeton and then coached for several years. He became a banker; he had a lot to do with the creation of a great group of banks in New York State known as Marine Midland. He was also in on the birth of Remington Rand and other big companies.

Yes, football does provide creative scrimmage for the players—particularly the quarterback—and for the coaches; but for us spectators, about all it does for our heads is to expose them to colds.

4.

As for water sports: swimming calls for a minimum of creativity. Water polo is analogous to basketball. Rowing, for most of the oarsmen, is mainly a matter of endurance and brawn. But, here again, the coach finds creative challenge in his job—even in rowing. John Collyer, president of B. F. Goodrich, is known as a giant both in judgment and in ingenuity. He pulled a never-to-be-forgotten oar at Cornell, and stayed on as coach. His experience in that job undoubtedly helped build up his brain power.

When we come to boating, Guy Lombardo tells me that it takes resourcefulness to win motorboat races the way he does. Such contests call for strategy, of course. However, the main use of imagination seems to be in designing the craft, and in devising ways to soup up the motors.

Leisurely sailing calls for no creative exertion. However, when the water is calm and the breeze is light, this pastime can be ideal for meditation. Einstein is said to have regarded non-competitive sailing as conducive to creative contemplation.

In sailing races, the skipper faces an intense creative challenge. Of course, instinct plays a big part; but even during a race there is time for deliberate cerebration—time enough to think up in advance whether, and at what time, to take the next tack, and all that. Herbert L. Stone has put his finger on this power of anticipation as a vital factor in successful yacht racing.

As editor of *Yachting*, Mr. Stone also stresses the use of imagination in the development of new and more efficient rigs for yachts in line with airplane-wing innovations. W. P. Carl of New York is a pioneer in "sails without masts." His experiments in this field are a model of imaginative thinking.

5.

Ollie Howard, who broadcasts each week about angling, has this to say: "Many of the uninitiated think of fishermen as stupids with nothing in mind except 'How many fish can I catch?' On the contrary, more creative imagination is used in fishing than in any other sport. From the Stone Age, when survival itself depended on the imagination of primitive man, to this modern day of self-appointed Izaak Waltons, success in the pursuit of fish has depended on the ability of the angler to use his creative wits."

Here again vicarious imagination is called for at every turn, even as to how to hold the line and when to give it a jerk. Dale Casto, on a deep-sea fishing expedition, was catching no fish; yet the man next to him was pulling them in hand over fist. "How come?" asked Dale, and his neighbor replied: "When you fish, you have to think like a fish. You have to put yourself in the fish's shoes."

Vicarious imagination is also needed to pick out the spot to fish. Alan Ward tells me: "When I go fishing I'm continually figuring what I'd do if I were a fish. I know that Canadian bass prefer cold water. So during a long calm hot spell I look for them where it's deep. That's where I'd be if

I were a fish. And that's where they are. When a storm churns up the lake and makes the surface cold, I fish on top."

The matter of bait also calls for imagination. For years the famous bonefish, in Florida waters, was thought to be allergic to flies. Then, a few years ago, an "ignorant" fly-caster thought up a technique which proved the opposite. The bonefish are now rising to flies the way they have probably been willing to do since time began.

A rich field for ideation is thinking up new kinds of bait. A friend of mine makes all his own lures. Tin cans, shoe-horns, tablespoons and thimbles stimulate him to wilder and wilder creations.

Tying flies is a creative hobby. In spite of the fact that fish are supposed to be color-blind, one addict devised over 100 colored concoctions. At his death his widow gave his collection to an old fishing buddy. But he never even tries those flies, because he prefers to develop new and better inventions of his own.

Ingenuity is also called for in thinking up fish-tempting substitutes. For instance, those who wade Catherine Creek for trout were set back on their heels when the New York State Conservation Department outlawed the use of trout eggs as bait. Imagination rushed to the rescue. Gum drops were cut up and rolled into tiny balls to simulate trout eggs. Vaseline was chilled and formed into globules. Then a die-hard devised a small mesh sack, holding a score of tapioca balls, cooked to the right consistency and dyed to a pinkish-yellow with Mercurochrome. This worked like a charm. To-day Catherine Creek rainbows are falling for tapioca, and trout fishermen have erected a mythical monument to the power of man's imagination.

Fish can smell in more ways than one. They use their noses in search of food. So now perfume is catching fish galore. A Knoxville fisherman named Davis thought it up. He calls it "Doodle Oil." You put it on your lure or bait. R. S. Thomas used two lines with the same worms on both.

But he perfumed line A with Doodle Oil and left line B odorless. Line A brought in a huge mess of big fish. Line B never got a nibble.

6.

Some of my closest friends would rather hunt than eat. I never realized how many of us feel this passion until a Detroiter told me that on the first day of deer hunting, over 400,000 men took to the woods in Michigan—more armed men in this one state than we had in Korea during that same fall of 1950.

My creative friends in the shooting fraternity assure me that hunting challenges imagination to the limit. My main informant was my late colleague Stan Irvin. To prove that "hunting is a battle of wits with alert opponents," he told me about a deer hunt in the mountains when the ground was covered with snow. His party of 10 regularly divided itself into six drivers and four watchers. For two days they made two drives daily. Examination of the snow after their sorties showed fresh deer tracks, both to the right and left of where they had stalked. The deer were simply turning, circling by them, and returning to their original beds. The men then thought up the idea of hiding downwind, to catch the beasts on their way back. This maneuver yielded a couple of shots, both misses.

After several such days, the deer seemed to have left the area. Again the men put their heads together and tried to outthink the dumb animals. Their best hunch was that the deer had gone into open country. So they embarked in a limousine and started to cruise. Sure enough, they found a contented buck leisurely moving through a bushy meadow. Two minutes later, they were sure of their venison dinner. "That was the only time on our trip that we out-thought the deer," said Stan.

My friends tell me that pheasants probably tax the

hunter's ingenuity more than any other game bird. You watch them head down a corn row, and then discover to your amazement that they have back-tracked and come out of the field behind you. Both the dogs and their masters are often outwitted by these allegedly slow-thinking, slow-moving fowl.

Lots of creative thinking and craftsmanship go into decoys, especially decoys for duck and geese. One instance of ingenuity along this line had its setting near James Bay where the North Country meets the Arctic. That's where geese have their breeding grounds. In the fall this silent land of the midnight sun begins to hum, then chatter, and then vibrate with the drumming wings and the hoarse cries of myriads of geese—just before they take off for the South. That's when sportsmen from all over the world congregate at Moose Factory, obsessed with bagging their share of these birds.

The hunters have to fly there by plane. Weight is a major problem, so they can't bring decoys; and wildfowl hunting without decoys is futile. "How can these geese be lured?" That was the problem. And an Indian thought up the solution. He dug clay from a pit, covered the top of each clod with tissue paper, and inserted a stick at one end to look like a neck and a head. Even the smartest of the geese were fooled by these crude impersonations of their cousins.

o   o   o

As for all games and sports—sedentary or active—indoors or outdoors—we should chose the ones which challenge our creativity. And we should go at them with gusto and imagination. Thus even play can help us build up our minds.

Chapter 11

T R A V E L – in what ways can it
help creativity?

W E AMERICANS are on the move more than ever. The
tourist trade is already one of our four largest industries
and is still rising.

When Thoreau claimed to have "traveled a good deal in
Concord," he meant, of course, that within a few acres he
had observed much and had imagined more. In a more literal
way another man, a century later, "traveled a good deal
in Concord." This was Harry Dooley, who spent several
years as spieler on a sight-seeing bus covering the same
locale.

From that start, Dooley built up the Gray Line Sight-
Seeing Companies, which conduct tours in so many of our
cities that their fares now total over $50,000,000 a year.

On escorted tours like those, the sight-seers enrich and
enliven their minds. They go because they seek the kind of
knowledge that feeds imagination. Their appetites make for
good ingestion. "For always roaming with a hungry heart,
much have I seen and known." So wrote Tennyson.

There is a carry-over value in almost any kind of travel.
The high spots linger long in our memories and strengthen
our power of association—so much so that, years later, we
may give birth to an idea that would not have come to us
had we not gone somewhere and seen something.

2.

Solitude in the high places has been recommended by many creative thinkers. Dr. Norman Vincent Peale holds that for creative meditation "there is nothing like peace-drenched mountains with their deep, sun-bathed, pensive valleys. . . . Here our minds clear, and our ability to think creatively returns."

Jesus Christ, when confronted with His direst problem, "withdrew into the hills alone."

Winston Churchill recommends a similar solitude, but not for mere meditation, and not necessarily in the uplands. His advice is: "Go to a peaceful spot, and stay there long enough to paint some canvases. . . . Every country where the sun shines, and every district in it, has a theme of its own. . . . Even if you cannot portray it as you see it, you feel it, you know it, and you admire it forever."

3.

Even our short motor trips can yield creative exercises, if we so will. Those little tours with our children on Sunday afternoons can be turned into creative pastimes, as has been proved by the Rindges of Silverlee Farm. When they take these drives, they play a game in which they try to describe what they see—not in terms of literal description, but rather by association.

"Freddie, what does that valley make you think of?"

"Well, Mother, it reminds me of the quilt on Tommy's bed—the way the fields are laid out."

"It's like our colored blocks, side by side," pipes up seven-year old Johnny.

A white-puffed cloudy day is a source of endless imagining for the Rindges—full of Indian chiefs, buffalo, birds and fish. A sunset becomes "a strawberry soda, turning finally to chocolate."

When they are driving in states where license plates carry two letters such as in EM–722, here's a game another pair of parents play with their two youngsters: They take turns working out a name for each plate on each passing car—a name which might fit its owner. So EM–722 might be "Evinrude Morkle," XY–659 might be "Xavier Yclept," and so on—the loonier the better.

"The only fault we find with that game," said the father, "is that it's so hard to stop. I keep on inventing names to myself every time I see a car until I almost go crazy. If I saw FFV, I'd probably yell out: 'Feterans of Foreign Vars.'"

Even when motoring on business we can use our minds creatively. Personally, I drive with a yellow pad alongside me, and I often stop and make notes. More than that, I frequently assign to myself a creative problem which I energetically brainstorm as I drive. I can't do this in city traffic, of course; but on long stretches it is safe. And it surprisingly shortens the trip.

More and more men who motor on business are carrying dictating machines in their cars—mainly for after-hours use. One man I know pulls up alongside the road now and then and dictates a memo on the spot.

When driven by a chauffeur, you can really step up your mental R.P.M. en route. One executive who travels many miles between home and office has installed in his car a hinged table at which he labors as if he were at his desk. In winter, a lamp illuminates his work on his way home. He has asked me not to divulge his name, but his creative record is nationally recognized.

4.

It is strange how few people ever seem to be doing anything on planes or trains. Nearly everybody seems to be idling. Vice-President Alben Barkley is typical. When asked what he did on long trips he replied: "I have no set way to spend my time on a train. I like to talk and relax with friends I see, or with some person who recognizes me."

Planes and trains are good places to think things up. Many an inventor, while traveling, has landed ideas he had sought in vain in his laboratory. At least a dozen chapters of this book were thought up and roughed out on my trips on planes and trains.

Asked about her literary work, Cornelia Otis Skinner replied: "When I actually do most of my writing is during a theatrical tour, and the place is in either a train or a hotel. Give me a long journey and the closed door of a bedroom or compartment, and I can turn out reams of stuff. Nor do I depend upon the cellular privacy of Mr. Pullman's swankier accommodations. I can write with ease in a day coach and I have even learned how to decipher the hieroglyphics produced by the roadbed of the Long Island."

But you don't have to be a professional writer to get more out of traveling by using your pen as you go. One of our office girls reported this:

"While on a trip to the Canadian Rockies last summer, I made memos as we went along on trains, on planes, on buses. Every night I transcribed these into my diary. My girl friends often said they couldn't see anything to write about; but the more I wrote, the more of interest I could see. I also found time to take snapshots, and chose each view with a particular friend or relative in mind."

My partner, Bruce Barton, circled the globe many years ago. He kept a diary, not only of his experiences, but also of the ideas he thought up each day. This record greatly enhanced the carry-over value of that trip. I have often seen him pick up that diary and pluck from it some thought of his for use in the weekly editorials which he wrote for more than 50 newspapers throughout the country, as well as for use in his books and magazine articles.

You can even compose music while traveling. Meyerbeer, who dreamed up most of his operas on trains, claimed that the clickety-clack of the wheels inspired him. And according to Robert Lewis Taylor, the famous pianist Percy Grainger, as he rides the rails from recital to recital, "does a lot of his composing on trains. He sings and hums and whistles to clarify things in his mind." Such creative activity would be mildly noteworthy if done in a Pullman. But Grainger always rides in day coaches, where concentration is well-nigh impossible, and where singing, humming and whistling would attract a jibing crowd of fellow passengers.

A woman I know, about to spend 10 hours in a day coach with her two young sons, dreaded the way they would bombard her with: "Mother, what will I do now?" So she told them at the start: "Here are two pads and pencils. Write down everything that you can think up to do on a train ride. I will give you a dime for each good idea you list." As a result, she paid her 10-year-old $2.30 and her seven-year-old $1.20. I have seen the 35 ideas they thought up. Some of them are worth putting into pamphlets for distribution on trains.

5.

A type of travel which forces imagination into play at every turn is the kind advocated by Episcopalian Bishop Edward R. Welles. His wife and he, last summer, took their four children on a camp-as-you-go trip to Alaska. In discussing that experience, Mrs. Welles remarked: "The more you depend upon yourself, the better able you are to think up ideas. That is one reason the Bishop and I chose to travel with our family the way we do—to out-of-the-way places and in a rough-it-as-we-go manner. We believe that this kind of travel has helped develop imaginative strength, not only in our children, but also in us parents. And luckily so, because we adults are far more in need of such creative stimulation than are our young."

In Alaska, the 13-year-old daughter, finding no sodas along the road, was content to feast on canned peas covered with tomato soup. "Why don't you cook like this at home?" she asked her mother.

When the Bishop's wife was stricken with mumps, she almost enjoyed her quarantine. She told me: "It was thrilling to lie on a mattress in our station wagon and revel in the ever-changing beauty of the Canadian Rockies across the aqua blue of Muncho Lake."

She had taken along a folding chair and an easel; but after her first try at doing a canvas on the Alcan, she found painting from the driver's seat the best way to outwit the mosquitoes. Her daughter sometimes sat on the hood of the car to do her water colors.

Late one summer afternoon, at our cottage in Canada, we welcomed a station wagon crammed with two parents, six children, and equipment for a transcontinental tour. The family was that of Professor Kenneth Sherk, he being on his sabbatical leave from Smith College. They were on their way to Alaska *and* Hawaii—all eight of them, with the youngest hardly old enough to toddle.

A year later I quizzed Mrs. Sherk about that trip. "It certainly is true that a terrific amount of creative power is generated during a travel expedition like that," she told me. "Our team of eight soon got so skillful that we could turn a good shade tree into a home—complete with kitchen, bedroom and playground—in 30 minutes flat."

Instead of playing with toys, the little ones became road builders and village planners. Out of sand or clay they constructed Diamond Heads and volcanoes. The trees they sketched were palms and redwoods, instead of the maples they always drew back home.

One child had had a few piano lessons but had never tried to write any music of his own. "One evening, a moose stamping into the dusky woods of Idaho inspired him to sit down and compose a piece," reported his mother.

"As for Mother," said Mrs. Sherk, "I learned many new arts. For instance, after having dragged an unwieldy vacuum cleaner around our home for many years, I had to discover how to sweep with a broom."

What schoolrooms of ingenuity those covered wagons of a century ago must have been! That source of creativity can now be somewhat recaptured by the kind of travel which the Bishop and the Professor provided for their families. And as welders of family ties, what other experiences could hold a candle to such expeditions?

6.

When we work our way as we travel, we cannot fail to exercise imagination. I saw the effect of this on a young man who, after three years in the Army, decided to rub war out of his memory by traveling on his wits. He had funds to go de luxe, but he chose instead to hitchhike his way across the country.

In Nebraska he joined up with a circus as an electrician. His experience for that job was nil. But he quickly picked up the little knowledge needed, and he stuck it out, on one-night stands, throughout the summer. He went back to college with his mind packed with firsthand experiences—a rich store of fuel for his imagination to draw upon as long as he lives.

Personally, I like to run out of money when on the road. Some of my most memorable experiences have come from finding my purse empty, with a long distance to go. In my twenties I learned, one evening, that I had to see Sir Wilfred Laurier in Montreal the next day. I was in Toronto at the time and knew of no one from whom I could borrow. I boarded the train and arrived at Montreal. While there I succeeded in raising enough funds to pay back the conductor of the Toronto-Montreal Express, and thus recover my gold watch.

Vagabonding has made many a man far more creative than he otherwise would have been. One outstanding example of this was Eugene O'Neill. He worked his way all over South America and across the Atlantic. Thus, by the time he was 24, he had stored up a mountain of rich ore, out of which his imagination could refine the gold with which his plays are laden.

7.

Excursions into outlandish places stretch imagination to the limit. I saw the result of such travel on my friend Daniel Streeter. When he retired as a manufacturer, he explored parts of the world where few white men had ever been. After several years of that, he settled down as an author— and as a citizen whose creative leadership will long be remembered by his community.

Lowell Thomas is another who has built up his imagination by meanderings off the beaten paths. His most sensational trip was to forbidden Tibet with his son. The book which Lowell, Jr., wrote about that can't fail to stir the reader's imagination. Just think what those firsthand experiences must have done to strengthen the imaginative muscles of the Thomases!

The whole world was in suspense after Lowell, Sr., was smashed up on the way out of Tibet. I thought to myself at the time, "Well, that probably means the end of this man's travels." But no! A few months later I wrote him and asked him how he was getting along. Here is part of his reply: "I've been up to Alaska doing a little skiing, mountain-climbing, and crevasse-jumping, on the great Juneau icecap." And Lowell was well over 50 at that time.

Even traveling in the wilderness—as in the Canadian woods—can provide plenty of creative exercise. It raises problems which must be solved right then and there by one's own ingenuity. Many such cases of inventiveness are recited in Horace Kephart's *Camping and Woodcraft*. Here's a sample:

"The toothache, scourge of the wilderness, Mr. A. W. North cured in a novel way. With a thread and a sheet of writing paper he made a cornucopia, the open end of which he placed flat upon a dish. He then set fire to the upper end of the cornucopia, whereupon the burning paper generated a drop of yellow liquid. This liquid—it is extremely bitter—he applied, with a toothpick and cotton, to the cavity; and the toothache perished amid the howls of the possessor of the tooth."

* * *

Whether our travel be "out of this world," or into the suburbs, it does add to our experience; thus it adds to the knowledge out of which imagination can generate ideas. It also steps up our automatic power of association. Travel likewise tends to open our minds, and thus, too, makes for ideation.

As a creative exercise its value depends upon whether it is the kind of travel which forces us to use ingenuity, and it also depends upon how we travel—whether we just go through the motions, or whether we put imagination into play all along the way.

Chapter **12**

HOBBIES – which ones should

we ride for creative exercise?

S AID SIR WILLIAM OSLER: "No man is really happy or safe without a hobby, and it makes precious little difference what the outside interest may be." But it does make a difference. Hobbies definitely vary in the degree of creative exercise they offer. Surely we should choose the ones which not only keep us happy, but which also help build up our minds.

What good does it do our imagination for us to make a fetish of super-accuracy with a rifle? One of many such hobbyists is D. A. Robbins, of Rixford, Pennsylvania. He has practiced to a point of being able, from 100 yards away, to pump 80 successive shots into a circle smaller than a quarter.

Or how creatively helpful can it be to practice perfectionism and patience as did Lee Fowler, Jr., of Highland Mills, New York, who spent four years building a replica of his grandfather's home out of 9000 toothpicks?

Any such single hobby may narrow rather than develop our minds. That's why A. Edward Newton recommends: "Get a pair of hobbyhorses that can safely be ridden in opposite directions." Many of our creative giants of literature have kept stables of such steeds. Victor Hugo not only made furniture; he also invented furniture. He not only painted pictures, but delighted in turning a blob of ink, while still wet, into a fascinating design. One of these rapid-fire creations of his is a black spider in a web, with infinitesimal demons crawling up the strands.

The all-time high in hobbies was depicted by Moss Hart and George Kaufman in *You Can't Take It With You*. Mother is writing a drama she started eight years before; one daughter is painting "The Discus Thrower"; another is making a mask of Eleanor Roosevelt. Other hobbies in the play include snake-collecting, stamp-collecting, toe-dancing, printing, dart-throwing, concocting confections, making fireworks in the cellar, and building a miniature model of a transatlantic power plant.

In actual life, many of our stage people are hard-riding hobbyists. Galina Talva, of *Call Me Madam,* carves statuettes out of soap while waiting backstage. Dancer William Weslow, of the same show, draws exotic birds. Naomi Riordan's hobby is sketching other members of *The Country Girl* cast. Brik Tone, of *Gentlemen Prefer Blondes,* creates masks and figurines. Dell Parker composes song lyrics instead of twiddling her pretty fingers.

In vocational guidance, aptitude-testers give weight to a person's hobbies. And rightly, because such interests can indicate the kinds of work most likely to be congenial. When personnel directors of big companies try to pick people of creative potentiality, they often find the hobbies of an applicant to be most revealing.

2.

Out of the 400 hobbies listed by Earnest Elmo Calkins, more than half have to do with acquiring, rather than creating. Most of these collecting hobbies tend to build knowledge and train judgment, rather than to stimulate imagination.

For instance, scouring a beach for shells does call for some knowledge; and as a bending exercise, it is a healthful hobby. But as a creative exercise, shelling rates low.

On the other hand, collecting autographs can call for resourcefulness. Some celebrated signatures are easy to acquire. Bing Crosby, for example, has set up a system which makes his autograph automatically available. In contrast, I saw several people try in vain to persuade Babe Ruth to sign their programs at an all-star game, where, for his first time, he was out of uniform. It would have taken superhuman resourcefulness to secure his autograph while he sat in his box-seat on that dismal day.

A high-school sophomore in Washington strains his ingenuity tracking down athletic stars in hotels. Some of his quarries regard him as a pest, while others like his initiative so much that they invite him to stop and chat. Another young friend of mine writes individual letters designed to get under the skin of the notables. I saw the one he wrote to the Duke of Windsor, and it was a masterpiece. Can you imagine any better creative practice than this boy derives from that hobby?

To think up a new collecting hobby is a creative triumph. Joseph Nathan Kane did just that with illustrious success. Starting 25 years ago to gather authentic "firsts," he discovered that, in many cases, originations had been wrongly credited. He proved that Fulton did not invent the first steamboat, that Remington was not the father of the typewriter, and that the Wright Brothers were not the first to fly a heavier-than-air machine. Kane's hobby has since become a business which yields him about $25,000 a year. As often happens, his avocation became his vocation.

Dorothy Blake also thought up a collecting hobby of her own—one which lifts her "out of the dark-blue dumps caused by reading the headlines of assorted kinds of villainy that seem to be roaming the world." Her hobby is poking through newspapers for news about "kindly people who have gone out of their way to lend a hand and spread a little extra happiness around." Her collections strengthen faith in the human race.

3.

By and large, handcrafts provide creative exercise to a greater degree than collecting. There seems to be a reciprocal influence between brain activity and manual activity of the right kind. According to Alfred North Whitehead, "The disuse of handcraft is a contributory cause to the brain-lethargy of aristocracies."

That principle helps to explain my admiration for my young friend Ted Hengerer, whose forebears owned huge stores. When Ted came out of World War II he decided to be a neighborhood baker. He made most of his bread and cake and rolls with his own hands. Meanwhile he developed an ever brighter personality, enlivened by a mind that sparks ideas. I quizzed him about combining headwork with handwork. He mused, "Well, it never occurred to me before, but I guess I do do some of my best thinking while kneading dough."

Handcrafts do more for us creatively if and when we think up the designs as well as carry them out. This is true of basket-making, embossing, wood-carving, metal working, modeling, and a score of other such crafts. Turning scrap into something useful or ornamental likewise challenges creativity. A book by Evelyn Glantz showed 401 worthwhile objects she had produced from odd pieces of wood, paper, cloth, bottles, boxes, and other pieces of junk.

Peter Hunt has inspired many of us to take on the hobby of remodeling secondhand furniture. He offers these pointers: "The first step is to disregard an object's original use. Approach it with a blithe spirit and an adventurous eye. Take it apart, change its proportions, reassemble it into something quite different, paint and decorate it as you wish— you'll end up with a piece that would grace any home and you'll have the time of your life doing it."

With the guidance of Hunt's *Workbook*, anyone can

"make something out of nothing," and in so doing can find a happy and profitable outlet for creative energy.

We can vigorously exercise imagination by trying to think up new things to create with our hands. A follower of Peter Hunt devised an article so popular that she now makes it by the dozen. It's a piece of wood in the shape of a Yale key about a foot high. Equipped with hooks to hold keys, each hook is labeled to identify each key.

Recently I walked through the glassmaking department of General Electric's chief research laboratory during the lunch hour. A young man was at "work" making a ship model out of glass. That's his hobby. What a stiff training for his imagination—to think up his designs and then, at every turn, to invent ways to make sails and spars and ropes out of molten silica!

Handwork is a basic principle of occupational therapy. If this be of a creative type, it tends not only to calm the nerves, but also to bring about a glow of self-realization. The value of handcraft as a healthful pleasure has often been stressed by Peter Hunt. "The happiest people," he claims, "are those who make things with their hands." And usually, through such recreation, they are helping to make themselves more creative.

4.

Some manual hobbies are supposedly for men, and others for women. But the sexes will not stay put. For example, Miss Elizabeth Armstrong rides sidesaddle the ladylike hobby of weaving; but she also straddles male hobbies such as metal working and toolmaking.

And it was a man who took up home tailoring when his baby caught cold from kicking off her bedclothes. This feminine handcraft of his resulted in a new sleep-suit that led to a new manufacturing success. His "Sleepy-Bye" garments are now sold everywhere.

When you think up something new to make, you intensify the creative value of any handcraft, even sewing—as when a wife solved a problem arising from the fact that her husband brought home too many dead deer each fall. She hit upon the idea of making gloves out of the hides. This annual hobby of hers takes headwork as well as handwork. And it removes a source of friction between her and her hunter husband.

More women engage in knitting than in any other handcraft. I often envy this occupation; it induces the kind of tranquillity that invites the muses. And it can activate creativity if the knitter tries to think up new designs and new techniques—as did Ethel Goetz Evans. She made a career out of knitting. The ideas she originated became the basis of lucrative books. In the last war she served as official designer of knit goods for the armed forces. President Franklin Delano Roosevelt was one for whom she personally created exclusive sweaters.

5.

Now for a few of the he-man hobbies so hard to ride that they provide creative exercise. For instance, a young friend of mine puts his savings into automobiles of ancient vintage. But he does more than collect them. He devotes his Saturdays to devising ways to make the old wrecks run. Were he trained in mechanical engineering, this hobby would call for acquired knowledge rather than for imagination; but with no technical background, he has to solve each puzzle from scratch.

Charles Kettering's hobby was research. After he retired from General Motors he started a lab in his cellar. Over 20 helpers came to work with him each day in his private home at Dayton.

William Stout, one of Henry Ford's original engineers, directed three research laboratories in Dearborn, Michigan; in his home, he conducted what he called his "screwball shop." For his grandson he turned out playthings such as cannon that shot Ping-pong balls. And he wrestled with highly scientific problems, such as a way to revolutionize flight—an idea so radical that he kept it secret lest he be laughed at.

No wife would applaud such uses of her home; nor would she clap her hands over the enterprise of Andrew C. Heckenkamp. He flooded his basement, not for swimming, but for experimenting with pearl-growing. He dug up mollusks from a nearby river, stuck sand-like particles into their flesh, and left them in the cellar until they frothed at the mouth and gradually built up pearls. He has had enough success with this hobby to warrant his hope that his cellar might turn out to be a mint.

Ralph Lee of General Motors is a man of many hobbies. He flies his own plane and his own glider. He has invented instruments for air navigation. He plays the pipe organ and the piano; he has composed accepted music. His etchings have been acclaimed by critics. But his outstanding avocation is casting metal.

For that pastime he has built, next to his home, a small but complete foundry, forge, and pattern shop. Here he spends his spare time producing castings, some as heavy as 75 pounds. Always trying to discover new and better ways to turn them out, he puts his creative best into this hobby. Thus he keeps building up his imaginative muscles, his physical sinews and his spirits.

6.

One dark winter morning, the villagers around Concord, New Hampshire, were awakened by bloodthirsty barkings. The dogs were trying to stop a stranger from forcing his way to back-stoop after back-stoop. This intruder was my friend Bayard Pope.

In New York City he strains his ingenuity every weekday helping to manage a huge group of banks. On week ends he runs his New Hampshire farm, well stocked with Ayrshires. While there he always wears work clothes because "so many unexpected things happen that you have to make a jack-of-all-trades out of yourself at the drop of a hat."

Late one afternoon, his man on the farm was rushed to the hospital, leaving nobody to milk the cows—nobody to deliver the milk to the 200 retail customers. And so, at three the next morning, it was Mr. Pope, the white-haired banker, who drove his truck out into the night to cover the route. In the pitch dark he found it tough to decipher where to deliver his bottles and how many. But his worst problem during those dark hours before dawn was to convince dog after dog that he was a milkman and not a marauder.

Many city men find farms to be creative challenges as well as sources of recreation. Some even run rural mills as hobbies. One such is Daniel B. Niederlander. A constructor of modern factories and skyscrapers, he spends his spare hours in the distant past as an old-time miller. For this pastime, he bought a mill which was first built in 1810. He brought century-old millstones from France. He re-dammed the creek to provide the power. He spends part of his week ends turning out old-fashioned flour for his friends. He tells me that this hobby of his is a continual challenge to his ingenuity.

A most spectacular large-scale hobby is the "North Pole Village" in the Adirondack Mountains. This idea was born about 15 years ago when Julian Reiss, about to retire from business, was asked by his little daughter, "What would it be like to visit Santa's workshop, Daddy?" He made up a story for her right on the spot. This ignited an idea which grew into a burning ambition. So he bought a tract of wilderness and turned it into a gay village made up of a dozen brightly colored houses, toymakers' shops, an iron forge, a glass-blowing establishment and a pottery—all centered around a lovely little home where a white-bearded Santa and his wife sit on the porch and greet the visitors.

The center of attraction is the "North Pole," a huge obelisk of real ice. To keep this frozen despite the summer sun, Mr. Reiss has installed a mammoth refrigerating plant.

The village is alive with bears and goats and deer. The 100 attendants are disguised as gnomes and elves. Over 300,-000 people visit there each year. *Admission* is free; but there is an exit fee of 80¢. Children under 10 and over 90, however, can come and go without charge.

7.

When we merely collect pets—whether they are fish or birds or snakes or cats or dogs or what nots—we train our imaginations but slightly. If, however, we stuff them, we engage in highly creative handcraft. For taxidermy requires a rare combination of skills such as sketching, painting, sculpture, model making, wax-working and woodworking.

The training of animals can provide more or less creative exercise—less if we go at it "by the book," more if we pit our own ingenuity against each problem the pet thrusts upon us. Dog-training, for example, can be routined on the principles of reward and punishment, in accordance with the 14 rules set forth by Will Judy in his *Training the Dog.*

An associate of mine, Joe Archbald, raised beagles in his cellar. Mrs. A. objected to their yelping during the night. So Joe thought up a solution. He put his pups in a box under the clothes chute. Then he ran a rope from his bed down through the chute, and tied a hammer to the nether end so that it rested on top of the packing case.

"Woof! Woof!" would go the little beagles. Joe, two floors above, would turn over in his bed, tug the rope, and "Bang! Bang!" would go the hammer on the pups' roof. Archbald would then dash downstairs, spank the pups, and yell "No! No!" in a devastating voice.

After a few such nights, Joe could just bang the hammer and stay abed—the pups would expect his arrival and keep quiet. This simple idea enabled Joe to train his beagles and also to restore marital harmony.

As one who believes in adapting ideas to new uses, I borrowed Joe's strategy in an effort to reform my 10-month-old grandson, who was visiting us for the summer. Night after night, his angry bawls would awaken us. We tried everything the child-training books told us to do; and nothing worked. So, one night after our umpteenth conference around the child's crib, I blurted, "This calls for a new idea. Leave this to *me*."

The next day I strung a cord from my bed, three rooms away, to a point right above the child's crib; and there I appended a sleigh bell. When he bawled, I tugged the string; the bell tinkled, and the child stopped crying. But soon he started up louder than ever. He quickly fell in love with the sound; he learned that, by crying, he could jingle the bell at will. This project is listed in Osborn's Creative "Triumphs" as Flop No. 397.

*　　*　　*

The net of it is that although nearly all hobbies are worth while, some provide more creative exercise than others—and the more imagination we put into these, the more mental good they can do us.

Chapter 13

FINE ARTS as sources

of creative training

THE FINE arts call for imagination—for "bringing something into existence," as Aristotle put it. This is true of music, sculpture, painting, and even aesthetic dancing.

Such activities can help nurture our creativity and undergird our happiness. They can even help integrate our characters, according to Arne W. Randall, of the U. S. Office of Education: "Art experiences are necessary to the development of a well-balanced individual."

The creative good we get out of an art depends, of course, on how we go at it. For example, when we passively listen to music we may set a mood for imagination; but when we are trying to compose, we actively exercise our creativity.

More and more amateurs are writing music. One of these is Eugene McQuade, a New York lawyer. While commuting, he often spends his time on the train trying to work up new scores. Another friend who composes is Lee Hastings Bristol, Jr. His middle name should be Versatility. For example, he can create and put on impersonations like a Cornelia Otis Skinner, and he can play the organ so well that he—an amateur—was recently invited to preside at the keyboard of the Cathedral of Notre Dame in Paris.

117

2.

Millions of us practice graphic arts, especially photography. This mainly calls for technical knowledge and judgment; hardly any of us ever put imaginative effort into our picture-taking.

Movie-making should be a creative workout for us amateurs; and yet most of us, including yours truly, are too prone to photograph whatever happens to come in our path. Were we to try deliberately to think up our subjects, our scenarios, and our captions, we could derive far more creative exercise from this hobby.

Painting and drawing can't fail to put imagination through its paces. We have to think creatively at every step from conception to completion. Sometimes an artist has to dream up the whole scene—as did Leonardo da Vinci when he imagined Christ and His twelve Apostles sitting at a table. To paint that picture da Vinci had to create, out of his mind, their dress, their features and the board at which they were convened.

Every stroke of brush, pen, or pencil tends to turn on that automatic power of ours called association of ideas. Eugene Speicher likened painting to playing with electricity. "Touch one part of the canvas," he said, "and something immediately happens to some other part. Part must be played against part until the whole acquires a state of living balance."

You may have seen at the Hotel Roosevelt in New York a dynamic executive named Paul Chatelain. I have often admired his resourcefulness—he can run a gigantic function as smoothly as if it were tea for two instead of an eight-course banquet for 1000. You ought to see his paintings.

"I paint every chance I get," he told me. "I believe that the hours I have spent at my easel have done a lot to build up the kind of imagination I need in order to think up fast the right solutions to the unpredictable problems which confront me day and night."

3.

Picture-painting, always a pastime of youth, has become a hobby of maturity. Harassed by the world's ills, many oldsters have found their best escapes to be landscapes. Winston Churchill recommends this hobby as "a mental exercise" and as an exciting satisfaction. In his *Painting As a Pastime* he wrote:

"To have reached the age of forty without ever handling a brush or fiddling with a pencil, to have regarded with mature eye the painting of pictures of any kind as a mystery, to have stood agape before the chalk of the pavement artist, and then suddenly to find oneself plunged in the middle of a new and intense form of interest and action with paints and palettes and canvases, and not to be discouraged by results, is an astonishing and enriching experience."

Anyone who can draw at all can paint; but it's safer to tackle oils than water colors. The latter have to be right the first time; the former can be worked over and over and over again.

In my first attempt I tried to depict our Christmas tree, with my grandson's teddy-bear sitting on a table. After two hours of effort, the evergreen looked like a bunch of asparagus and the animal looked like an over-sized potato. If I had been using water colors, that daub would probably have been my last. But, because I was working in oils, I could cover up my mistakes. I redid and redid that canvas until finally it became so good that the little boy's mother decided to frame it and hang it in his room. (The fact that she was my daughter in no way biased her judgment, of course.)

My second masterpiece was an oil of my residence. To block this in, I sat across the street in my car on a zero day and sketched a rough layout. Three days later I crossed the street again and compared my painting with my house—only to find that I had put two extra windows in the attic. Thanks to working in oils, this was easily corrected.

When I showed my first botches to a professional artist and asked him about taking lessons, he counseled: "Keep going on your own. If you take lessons you will expect too much of yourself, and you'll be less happy with what you paint. Then, too, the less you know about techniques, the more you'll have to blaze your own trails. And that will be fun."

Most of the daubsters I know didn't start till after 50. One of these is John Oishei, employer of some 6000 people, inventor of windshield wipers and other such devices. Without instruction, he became quite skillful. Then he took some lessons, and his latest work is almost worthy of an art gallery.

An oil painting of a skyline recently exhibited in New York was done by Zelig Tepper, who started to paint at the age of 71. Afflicted by cataracts, his sight is so impaired that he has to work with his right eye less than one inch away from the canvas. He began to paint only three years ago; and yet the works of this aged watchmaker are already acclaimed by critics. He is a male prototype of Anna Mary Robertson, who began painting at the age of 78 and is now known to multitudes as Grandma Moses.

Even if we have too little talent or courage to attempt portraits or landscapes, we can do folk art. "This," says Peter Hunt, "is the handcraft of people all over the world who naturally and without training in any of the fine arts discover an outlet for the innate desire to create and beautify things. . . . Usually their work is fine because they love doing it."

4.

Many would-be Whistlers just never can get started. One emotional block is what Joseph Alger has called "the unwarranted aura of awe which surrounds oil painting." In his book, *Get In There and Paint,* he proves that "anybody can do it."

Many start but soon quit, because they aim too high at first. Early attempts at portraits are often suicidal. It takes a real artist to make John Doe look like John Doe; but almost any of us can make a hill look like a hill, a house look like a house, and a tree look like a tree. Alger recommends a ketch-up bottle as an ideal starter.

We would-be painters should not look down on homely subjects, any more than did Rembrandt. Recently in New York, Lester Gaba, a sculptor, exhibited 15 paintings of vegetables. So many people crowded to see these that the queue was half a block long.

Some artists sneer at using photographs as aids to painting. We novices should ignore that prejudice. Most of us are so busy that we can paint only at home and at night. It's no mean achievement to take a tiny snapshot and transmute it into a canvas three feet wide, with all the coloring coming out of one's imagination.

One of New York's best portrait painters never asks any subjects to "sit" for him. He takes colored photographs and from these paints a composite. Norman Rockwell never hesitates to work from photos he has personally posed. Why, then, should we tyros try to limp along without crutches legitimately within our reach?

When all is said and done, the big thing is to make a start. So let's take a leaf out of Churchill's book: "Having bought the colors, an easel, and a canvas, the next step was *to begin.* But what a step to take! The palette gleamed with beads of color; fair and white rose the canvas; the empty brush hung poised, heavy with destiny, irresolute in the air. My hand seemed arrested by a silent veto. But after all the sky on this occasion was unquestionably blue, and a pale blue at that. There could be no doubt that blue paint mixed with white should be put on the top part of the canvas. One really does not need to have had an artist's training to see that. It is a starting-point open to all."

5.

To get the most creative good out of painting, we should steel ourselves against slavishness. Always we should keep our minds crackling with "What else?" "How else?" "What if?" For one thing, let's specifically try to think up ways to dramatize our portrayals.

Maurice Collette, a business executive, recently had a one-man exhibition at an exclusive gallery on 57th Street, New York. The hit he made was largely due to the imagination he had put into making each picture tell a story. One of his paintings depicted a farm scene. The ground was covered with snow; the setting sun looked cold. The center of interest was the farmer, driving his team of horses homeward. In actual size he was about as big as the end of a match. But you could almost see him shiver; and the slump of his posture told you how hard he had been working.

Even in redecorating furniture, we should try to dramatize. "Why not let the decorations tell a little story, no matter how remotely?" asks Peter Hunt. "It is all very well to have a little man and a little woman standing side by side, framed in a garland of hearts and flowers and birds. . . . But if the same little man is handing the same little woman a heart or a flower, and the owner's initials are painted above them or woven into place in the encircling garland, then a little personalized story is the result."

What a creative feat it is to picturize drab facts! Our hats are off to the cartoonists who do this every day.

The baseball standings show that the Brooklyn Dodgers are 10 games ahead. The date is August first, 1951. How can we turn these pale statistics into a colorful picture—in black and white?

One cartoonist did this with a pen-and-ink drawing of an

unshaved ball-player lolling in an exclusive club, bemoaning his lack of worthy foes, but recalling how in 1942 he had been thrown out of that charmed circle after being just as far in the lead on that same date—how he and his fellow "Bums" had muffed the pennant in the home stretch nine years before.

We might even try to be original in our techniques. Instead of slavishly doing as taught, it is more fun—and better creative exercise—when we think up our own ways of doing this or that. I sought falling snow as the setting of a portrait of my grandson. What to do to put some flakes out front and others in the background? Any teacher could probably have told me that secret. But what a kick I got out of finding out for myself! Then, too, on a landscape I tried to show a foreground of waist-high reeds, but they persisted in looking like short grass. I solved that by scratching vertical lines into the wet paint. What with? A golf tee.

6.

Those whose duties call for ideas still feel the need of other creative activities. Lilly Daché, the designer, is one of these. "Because I so thoroughly believe that imagination can be developed through exercise, I try to help my creativity in fashion by expressing myself in other forms, such as painting." Don Herold believes likewise. One of his favorite sayings is, "Minds need rotating as well as crops."

It is not only fun to shift from hobby to hobby, but the more hobbies we ride, the more versatile we become. And the better we can build our hedges against old age.

Now that our span of life is so much longer, more and more old people will have to face the problem of leisure. In New York City alone there are already more than 500,000 people over 65. Whether they live out their lives instead of dying out their lives will depend to some extent on their creative activities.

A neighbor of mine, long since retired, dropped in one Saturday afternoon while I was at my easel. He asked me some questions. Then, almost with tears in his eyes, he said, "Oh, what I would give to have a hobby like that!" Business was his only interest. He can't even read any more. He is sick of going to ball games. He has nothing to look forward to. If he had started to paint before too late, how much sunnier his twilight might have been!

In contrast, Peter Hunt cites his own father, who took up painting at 60. He started on a piece of cloth torn out of an old sheet—tacked to a frame dug out of a scrap heap. From then on, he painted nearly every day, all day long. He died at 64. Those four years, according to his son, "were the most gratifying and buoyant he ever had."

Our nation needs more creative hobbies like painting. Working hours have been cut to the point where free time can pose a problem even to those still in their prime. As inventive science takes over more and more of man's work, what will our people do with their ever greater leisure? Too many will just sit and hear or watch other people. How much better if they were to do something themselves—something like painting—which could help make them more content, more kindly, more *creative*.

Chapter 14

WORD PLAY can exercise our

creative wits

LET'S NOW LOOK into creative exercises of a rhetorical type. But let's not drop pictures quite yet; for the verbal and the visual often belong together. A picture can be worth 1000 words; by the same token, the more graphic our words, the better.

Most of the ad-makers try first to think up the idea, and then the illustration—tasks which call for much more creative effort than the writing of the text. Even when they are handed the words and asked to dream up illustrations, they have to turn creative somersaults.

For example, every Monday morning two copy-writers received a list of those songs which had scored highest in national popularity during the previous week—the songs which were to be televised on "Your Hit Parade" the following Saturday night.

Even with nearly 100 craftsmen working like mad to create that show, six days were hardly enough. That's why each Monday these men toiled far into the night. In the fewest possible hours they had to lay the foundation for that week's program by thinking up the right picture for every sentence, every phrase—yes, almost every word—in every one of those lyrics. Until these ideas were in hand, the many other craftsmen could not start on their specialized tasks.

Those two thinker-uppers performed that herculean feat regularly, week in and week out. What an example they set for the rest of us! They prove how much, *much* more creative power we could generate if we drove ourselves.

We might tear a leaf out of their book by tackling something comparable but far less hectic. How? By creating a rebus. Let's pick a paragraph, and then try to think up a picture for every salient word. Although this can be fun, it's a tough enough assignment to give any imagination a good workout.

2.

We activate our visual imagination even less when viewing television than when listening to radio. Some radio stars actually help their listeners to "see" as they hear. Jack Benny is outstanding in his ability to do just that—by means of his words, his inflections, and his timing. This bit typifies that skill:

Jack: "Take my hair, for instance."

(*Pause.* Here the listener thinks of a wig.)

Jack: "Put that back."

(*Pause.* Here, the listener visualizes wig in stooge's hand.)

Jack: "There!"

(*Pause*—Here, the listener "sees" the wig being put back on Jack's head.)

Jack: "Not so far over on one side."

(At this point, the listener laughs at how ludicrous Jack must look.)

Just as others can prompt us to visualize, so we can lead ourselves to exercise imagination by consciously running pictures through our own minds. Even tiny children can do this. My minister, in a talk to a class of four-year-olds, bade them close their eyes. A minute later, he asked them what they had seen while their eyes were shut. "Nothing" . . .

"Not a thing" . . . "Everything was dark." All the answers were in that same vein—all except one: "I saw what I was *thinking* about."

That from a four-year-old child was remarkable. But we grown-ups should know that we can *make* ourselves see what we *will* to see, even if we are blind. So let's make some slides for ourselves. Let's start with one word—an abstraction like *opportunity*. What symbols for that can we light up in our minds? A ladder, a stairway, a hill with the sun bursting over the horizon—the face of Lincoln or of Edison or of one of the many immigrants who have risen to fame in our country— these are but a few of the pictures we could create.

Or how about making a mental movie of the 23rd Psalm? "The Lord is my Shepherd." (Clearly we can see that bearded herder with his sheep.) "He maketh me to lie down in green pastures." (Vividly we can view those verdant acres on that hillside.) "He leadeth me beside the still waters." (You never saw a pool more placid. And just look at those lacy clouds mirrored on its surface.)

Some psychiatrists believe that this psalm as thus picturized can serve as a mental therapy. Such use of visual imagination most certainly can serve as a creative exercise.

3.

Let's go a-hunting for synonyms. Let's send our imagination in search of terser and brighter ways to say our say. Whatever we do to think up alternatives of any kind is always good creative practice.

Strangely enough, nearly all of our dim polysyllables were glowing phrases back in their original Latin and Greek. Take *acumen*. To us moderns, this word lights up no image. But to the Romans, the word acumen painted a picture of *needle-*sharpness.

It is not always true that the shorter the word the better. Abraham Lincoln was a master of terseness; and yet in his

Gettysburg speech of 271 words he used 71 polysyllables. No short word could take the place of *dedicate*.

Nor is it always true that the fewer words the better. "Sorry enough to quit." Doesn't that hit harder than "repentant"? *The New York Times* called a book "intelligent, realistic, eloquent." Although most lawyers lean toward labored words, Justice Owen Roberts said of the same book, "It strikes a telling blow for straight thinking." He used over twice as many words as *The Times*; but he penned a picture.

Synonym-hunting may sound like deadly calisthenics; but we can make this exercise exciting by turning it into a game. For example, a mixed group of all ages tried one evening to think up ways of saying "superficial." We hit upon 27 synonyms other than those listed in our thesaurus. One of the graphic words we thought up was "horseback." A "horseback survey" certainly paints more of a picture than does a "cursory survey."

That kind of game also makes a good twosome. My associates Dale Casto and Carl Davis set out jointly to think up synonyms for *acumen*. They knew that a professor and I had thought up 38; so Dale and Carl were bent on beating that mark. They won. In three hours (on a train) they listed 72 words, phrases and figures of speech meaning acumen—34 more than Professor Arnold Verduin and I had been able to dream up in the hour we had spent on the same project.

"No one who does not expend a good deal of care upon points of synonyms can write well," declared H. W. Fowler, co-adapter of *The Concise Oxford Dictionary*. He urges that we develop "the power of calling up the various names under which the idea we have to express can go. Everyone has this power to some degree. *Everyone can develop this gift through exercise.*"

4.

It makes a good stretching exercise to try to stretch synonyms into figures of speech. These can be as simple as those which a group of us thought up: "As superficial as a Bikini bathing suit" . . . "As superficial as a cat's bath." Or, they can include an ironic twist, as when Dorothy Parker likened superficiality to "running the gamut from *a* to *b*." In his book, *Teaching to Think,* Julius Boraas strongly recommended as a creative exercise any such effort to think up figures of speech.

Some of my daughter's friends make a foursome of that activity. Occasionally, before starting their bridge, one of them reads aloud from the page in *The Reader's Digest* called "Quips." Then each of the four thinks up and writes down at least three possible entries. Here are a few examples—none of them good enough to make the *Digest,* but all good enough to make the game interesting: "One cross we bear is being cross with each other" . . . "The most common of chronic complaints is complaining" . . . "Blessed are they whose children do not whine as they dine" . . . "When fools get tight, their morals get loose" . . . "Liquor turns some souls into heels."

5.

H. L. Mencken recommended that, for creative exercise, we take a crack at coining slang. Any such expression, to catch hold, must be imaginative; usually it paints a picture in a flash.

Slang often becomes literature. "Filthy lucre" came up from the gutter into the New Testament (*Timothy* III, 3). "By the skin of my teeth." That sounds like slang, but it is a classic figure of speech. (See *Job* XIX, 20.)

Authors who otherwise shun slang often put it into the mouths of their characters. Thus Thomas Mann in describing Artur Rubinstein's piano-playing quoted a teen-age youngster as exclaiming, "Boy! He plays from the socks up!"

The line between slang and figurative speech is as shadowy as a spider's thread. And Father Time often rubs out that boundary—as H. L. Mencken proved in *The American Language.*

"There is a constant movement of slang terms into accepted usage," he wrote. "The verb-phrase *to hold up* is now perfectly good American, but so recently as 1901 the late Brander Matthews was sneering at it as slang. In the same way other verb phrases, e.g., *to cave in, to fill the bill,* and *to fly off the handle,* once viewed askance, have gradually worked their way to a relatively high level of the standard speech. On some indeterminate tomorrow *to stick up* and *to take for a ride* may follow them."

Slang is wrongly supposed to sprout by accident from lowbrows and collegians. According to Mencken, most of it "is coined in the sweat of the brow." It comes from creativity at work.

So let's not be ashamed to emulate Ring Lardner. To think up slang is almost as respectable—and just as good exercise—as to think up figures of speech.

6.

The man who ate the first oyster needed less courage than I show here in speaking well of punning. The fact is that puns can serve as crossbars on which we can chin ourselves creatively.

Many of our literary lights have lauded this pastime. James Boswell claimed that "A good pun may be admitted among the excellencies of lively conversation." Charles Lamb went even further: "A pun is a noble thing per se. It fills the mind. It is as perfect as a sonnet; better."

Edgar Allan Poe put his finger on one reason why so many of us are thumbs-down on puns. Said he: "Those who most dislike them are those least able to utter them." About 100 years later Oscar Levant innocently paraphrased Poe by wisecracking: "The pun is the lowest form of humor—when you don't think of it first."

One just criticism of puns was brought out by Sydney Smith 150 years ago: "Puns are the wit of words. The wit of words is miserably inferior to the wit of ideas." Puns do fall short in that they depend too much on verbiage and too little upon imagery. For this reason, jokes based on word-play are seldom as funny as those based on humorous situations.

Puns are less likely to be pooh-poohed when used as a natural part of a message. A New York friend of mine never dares play upon words while at home lest his children boo him down. During December his daughter at college wrote him, "When I get home for Christmas vacation, I want to take a gander at *South Pacific*. Will you get me a ticket?" To which the father replied by wire: "No tickets available at any of the usual sources; so I am seeking a new source for your gander." Strangely enough she showed that telegram to her schoolmates with gleeful pride.

Those least in need of creative exercise are most likely to sharpen their wits on puns. Bennett Cerf is one of these; and he likes to collect pearls dropped by friends of his whom he calls pun-dits. Here are three of Cerf's favorites:

"At the conclusion of a brief discourse by Clifton Fadiman on the life of an old Turkish despot, John Gunther asked, 'Are you shah of your facts?' Fadiman snapped back, 'Sultanly.'

"Five-year-old Wylie O'Hara upon being introduced to a patched-up little girl from Montgomery began warbling, 'She Came from Alabamy with a Band-Aid on Her Knee.'

"A publisher who had lost his shirt on a succession of unsuccessful first novels complained, 'I'm suffering heavily from new-writus.'"

Throughout my life I have been blessed with friends with whom I could pun congenially. For example, in my early 'teens at Hamilton College I frequently engaged in this kind of mental sword-play with my classmate Alexander Woollcott. He was a master punster. I remember many of his double cracks. For example:

On a frigid morning we were walking up a steep hill. The sidewalk was packed solid with snow, but a bright sun made it sticky. Suddenly he slipped, having stepped on a shaded spot. He stopped, looked up at the tree, and exclaimed, "That must be a slippery elm."

A bit later, when he stepped on a similar shadow, I asked him, "Why didn't you slip that time?" Looking skyward he quickly retorted, "That must be an *ash*."

The usual pun is played upon a single word. It is more fun and better exercise to think up doubles, as Dizzy Dean did (consciously or otherwise) when he was told that his radio listeners were critical of his syntax. Diz exploded, "Sin tax? You don't mean to tell me they're putting a tax on that, too?"

Triple puns are even harder and quite rare. Here's one that Bill Feather liked well enough to call to my attention: "E. W. Hornung, brother-in-law of Sir Arthur Conan Doyle (creator of Sherlock Holmes), had this to say about his relative's hero: 'Though he might be more humble, there's no police like Holmes.'"

If you agree that punning is good exercise for one's imagination, my suggestion is that you pick a pun-loving pal and take him on long walks. While thus engaged, the two of you can play upon words with less embarrassment and more enjoyment.

7.

We can creatively thrive on conversation, but it must be of the right kind. The usual "I-hear-the-Smiths-are-separating" type of chit-chat can't even massage our minds.

Spirited discussions of worth-while subjects help in two ways. They enrich our memories with material which nurtures our imaginations, and they make us think creatively. Even as we speak, we have to plan what to say later on. And we have to imagine in advance what our companion is about to say. Such catch-as-catch-can exercise helps develop our creativity.

Our forebears sharpened their wits by arguing issues. We too often let columnists and commentators make up our minds, with the result that the practice of debating—of "disagreeing agreeably"—no longer spurs our ingenuity.

Radio and especially television have done much to kill conversation. Contract bridge likewise uses up many hours which otherwise might be spent in profitable talk.

But, again, those least in need of creative exercise still cross verbal swords. For example, one morning I asked my partner, Bruce Barton, what kind of time he had had the night before. I knew he had dined and spent the evening with Grantland Rice and with Burton Peek, head of Deere & Company. Bruce's reply went something like this:

"I didn't get to bed till almost three this morning. If I told you what I did during those nine hours you wouldn't believe me."

"What did you do?"

"I just sat all that time with that sports columnist and that manufacturer of manure spreaders while we discussed Shakespeare."

8.

Public speaking can be a potent exercise; it forces our creative minds to go all out, in preparation and delivery. No saying was ever truer than that spoken by Erasmus: "By speaking men learn to speak."

My friend Richard E. Borden was once a tongue-tied professor. He disciplined himself into becoming a speaker; and by practice he grew to be one of the nation's platform stars. He will tell you, as he told me, that in driving himself to that end he developed himself creatively to the point where several manufacturers were glad to pay him highly for his consultive services.

Dale Carnegie could have told those who take his speaking courses that, in addition to learning to talk on their feet, they are also strengthening their creative wings. They most certainly are training themselves to put forth effort, and effort is the motor of imagination.

Formal debate is likewise a strenuous exercise. This certainly calls for the utmost in catch-as-catch-can creativity. The very preparation strains imagination because, for one thing, no debater can win unless he first puts himself into his opponent's shoes and anticipates the arguments he will have to rebut.

On that point, here's what my minister, Dr. Butzer, told me out of his own experience: "In college debating we always had to prepare both sides of every question. In triangular debates, each of the three colleges would have a negative and an affirmative team to oppose its rivals. To prepare for these contests our own two teams would hold several preliminary debates between them. Many of us felt that these efforts provided us with more creative training than anything in our curriculum."

Dr. Butzer went on to remark that in his opinion the high creativity of Abraham Lincoln was at least partially due to his early practice in forensic dueling.

       ❋   ❋   ❋

Public speaking and public debating are probably beyond the opportunity and the power of many of us. But all of us can dream up pictures, can hunt for synonyms, can think up figures of speech. And through such rhetorical exercises, we can lift our minds to higher creativity.

Chapter 15

WRITING is mental wrestling

at its best

W HEN WE WRITE we have to grapple, not only with words, but also with theme, sequence and syntax. Without doubt we can derive plenty of creative exercise from pushing a pen.

Scientific tests regard "facility in writing" as a basic index of creative aptitude. Arnold Bennett insisted that "the exercise of writing is an indispensable part of any genuine effort towards mental efficiency." Nancy Osgood, N.B.C. commentator, recently said to me: "I know of no better way to strengthen one's creative muscles than to sit down each day and write for an hour or so."

A young nephew of mine asked me how much a joke sells for, and I said the price varies from a dollar to $100.

"I'm going to write a $100 joke," he remarked.

"When are you going to start practicing?" I asked.

"Why do I need practice?" he bridled.

To encourage him, I offered him a dollar if he would write ten jokes for me.

"What! Only a dime apiece? Nix!"

That lad believes in practice when it comes to sport; but like many grown-ups, he doesn't appreciate the importance of practicing writing.

And then there is the fallacy about our needing to be

"born" writers in order to write. The truth is that every author was once an amateur. Matthew Arnold, a plodding school inspector, suddenly found himself hailed as a man of letters. Anthony Hope was a barrister named Hawkins. Joseph Conrad sailed before the mast for 16 years before he discovered he was a novelist. Conan Doyle, a physician, created Sherlock Holmes as a hobby. A. J. Cronin was likewise a family doctor, and so was Oliver Wendell Holmes. Charles Lamb clerked in India House, and started writing to overcome his boredom. Stephen Leacock taught at McGill University for many years before he found that his quill could tickle us. Longfellow was a language teacher. Anthony Trollope was a postal inspector. Herman Melville was an obscure customs official for 20 years before *Moby Dick* made him famous.

As Laurence Sterne stated nearly 200 years ago, writing is but a different name for conversation. If we can talk, we can write, provided only that we strive hard enough.

2.

Even if we never try to write professionally, there are many forms of amateur effort on which to sharpen our creative wits. Even letter-writing can provide helpful training if we go at it right.

A young associate of mine consciously reaches for ideas to enliven his correspondence. Instead of dashing off a routine recital of trivia he goes at each letter as if he were writing an article. Even such exercise can help keep us on our creative toes.

Why not try that? Or better yet, how about illuminating your words with pictures? See what you can do to illustrate your next epistle to that little friend or relative of yours. It will mean a lot more to the youngster, and it will be far better exercise for you. President Theodore Roosevelt continually practiced that kind of double-barreled creativity.

Almost every family could well publish its own private periodical. My old city editor, Mark Daly, now retired, keeps his mind toned up by typing out a family newspaper once a week for his children, grandchildren and friends. When some of my young kin first went away to college, we ran a family newspaper called *Scriblets*. I was the editor; but to every issue, each of the home-staying youngsters had to contribute. This was mighty good practice for them—as they later realized.

Or how about writing a book for fun? Betty Miller, a bank clerk, makes a hobby of doing a volume on each summer's sojourn. Her 10 books are salted with humor as well as filled with descriptions and pictures. "My friends tell me they can relive each trip with me," she told me with well-placed pride.

When your living-room table gets piled with Christmas greetings, aren't you amazed (as I am) that the stand-outs are those few which your friends have created on their own? For many years I have made it a practice to originate our family's holiday greetings. Nut that I am, I usually begin in January to file away ideas for our next Christmas card.

There are many other opportunities for amateur effort. One of my young friends practices by writing his own gag lines for magazine cartoons and sometimes tops the caption chosen by the editors. Another tears a picture from a magazine and writes a short story around it. A woman who is easily irritated by radio commercials occasionally rewrites one the way she would like to hear it.

An industrial engineer who had never written "anything" attended a course in creativity at the University of Buffalo. His instructor, Robert Anderson, asked him to write a story for children. I saw the manuscript which Boyd Payne turned out. It's a tale about a chicken—a Cinderella story entitled "Chickendrella." The scene is Coop Town. The main characters are Flossie Feathers and Brewster Rooster, who live on Cockscomb Avenue. It's a story that would delight any child.

It helps prove that nearly all of us have it in us to write—even though we have never written, and have never thought we could.

3.

How about taking a swing at rhyming, for fun and for exercise? Of all forms of versifying, the one that calls for the toughest of mental gymnastics is probably the limerick.

The alleged father of the limerick was Edward Lear, the author of "The Owl and the Pussycat." Present-day addicts charge, however, that he avoided the hardest part of limerick-writing by making his first line serve also as the last line, e.g.: "There was an old man of Tobago. . . . That naughty old man of Tobago."

A different last line is a "must" in most good limericks, and the best last lines are usually O. Henry-ish. Such "stoppers" can be phrases which illustrate unexpected pictures, or they can be puns as complicated as this:

> There was a young lady named Banker
> Who slept as the ship rolled at anchor
> She awoke with dismay
> As she heard the mate say
> "Let's haul up the top sheet and spanker!"

You can start a limerick with a malapropism, or an unusual rhyme, or a weird use of a word. Some of the best limericks are rhymed retellings of stories. Some are adaptations of old limericks. But we amateurs should try to adhere to the traditional form.

Let's emulate Oliver Herford, who made a hobby of limerick-writing. Let's play hide-and-seek with rhymes. To do this we must send imagination up alley after alley in search of ideas that will click and of words that will sound alike. Road work like that surely tends to flex our creative muscles.

4.

Ralph Satterlee recommends participation in prize contests. "For 20 years before I became a professional writer," he told me, "I strengthened my imaginative muscles by continually taking stabs at all types of competitions. I was one of the winners in over 550 of these contests, and my cash prizes averaged over $1000 a year."

He has urged schools to use such contests as class assignments. At Woodbury College, in cooperation with Professor Phelps Gates, he persuaded 500 students to enter a local department-store competition. They won 11 prizes, including all the top money. "The students were enthused," reported Satterlee, "and their imagination was fired. They did better work in their studies, and popped more ideas."

For similar practice swings why not contribute short pieces to magazines? Several periodicals issue standing invitations, especially *The Reader's Digest.*

For its feature, *Life in These United States,* the *Digest* offers $100 for each contribution of under 300 words. These items must be true, unpublished stories, based on your own experience, revelatory of adult human nature, and providing appealing or humorous sidelights on the American scene.

Likewise, for its *Humor in Uniform* department, the *Digest* offers $100 for each true and unpublished story based on experience in the armed forces.

For *Personal Glimpses, Laughter, the Best Medicine, Campus Comedy* and other anecdotal items, the compensation for original material is $10 per two-column line.

It's fun to think up these shorts. And it's excellent exercise. I know because I've tried it, at times successfully.

5.

Recent surveys tell us that nearly 2,500,000 Americans are trying to write for money, and this is just about the toughest of all creative exercises.

Many of those would-be writers will hope for too much too soon, and will fall by the wayside—stopped by discouragement. But many others will make out well over the long run, according to A. S. Burack, editor of *The Writer*. He estimates: "For every person who hits the jackpot in writing and achieves big money and fame, there are at least 30 or 40 who make comfortable incomes or supplement their earnings by writing a few hours a day."

In Polly Webster's *How To Make Money At Home*, editor Burack has a chapter which comprehensively covers the field of writing, and which can help guide us as to what kind of literature to tackle—whether factual, as for feature articles and non-fiction books—or fictional, as for short stories and novels. That chapter also covers humor, plays, and poetry.

Plenty of how-to books are available on any type of writing effort. *The Writer* publishes a list of 36 such works. Quite a few universities offer worth-while instruction, and there are correspondence courses which successfully teach techniques.

Some of the so-called Writers' Conferences are closed to all except professionals; but quite a few (including the outstanding Bread Loaf Workshop at Middlebury) are open to "auditors," to amateurs who wish to spend their summer vacations at such sessions. Every year *The Saturday Review of Literature* publishes a directory of these workshops.

One way to learn about techniques is recommended by Charles and Margaret Broadley, and this is to review published writings of the kind which we would attempt. By reading such work analytically, and then writing a review, we can do much to teach ourselves.

Nearly all writers agree that we should try to write only about that which we know best. William More advised: "Don't try to look up subjects for writing. The best subjects are already in your mind." Sir Philip Sidney admonished likewise: " 'Fool!' said my muse to me—'look in thy heart and write.' "

Again, the command is to get going. Any subject is better

than no subject. The versatile author and editor J. P. McEvoy told his children not even to worry about techniques, but to go ahead and write: "You'll never learn to drive a car by memorizing the names of the parts and drawing a diagram of the chassis. You learn to drive well by driving. You learn to write well by writing."

Many who want to write never do so because they are "too busy." Such people can't possibly have less time than Dr. William Carlos Williams. Day and night he calls on patients in a New Jersey community of industrial laborers. And yet this busy physician has gained fame as a poet and as author of countless short stories.

Several of my friends can write well enough to sell their wares; but when I talk to them about doing something for publication they panic. They rightly fear that the first piece they submit will be turned down by editors. They don't realize that these trial heats provide the practice which could turn them into stars.

Another road block is our queer quirk about "waiting for the mood." My boyhood home was near Fordham, where Edgar Allan Poe had lived. Local legend had it that he wrote only when it rained. Later I learned that he had once remarked that he seemed to write better on rainy days but that he did some writing every day, rain or shine. "I don't wait for moods," said Pearl Buck. "You accomplish nothing if you do that. Your mind must know it has got to get down to work."

6.

If little girls are made of sugar and spice and all things nice, what is writing made of? What else but ideas? The words are important, but only to clothe our thoughts.

The first big task is to think up the big idea. "To produce a mighty book you must produce a mighty theme," said Herman Melville.

It was the *idea* that made a classic of Charles Lamb's

Dissertation on Roast Pig. A pigsty went up in flames. A Chinese swineherd raked the embers with his hand, licked his fingers, and found the taste delicious. This led to an epidemic of pigsty-burning—until someone found that pig could be toothsome even if roasted on a tame fire, instead of on a flaming pigsty. Lamb's theme was a simple switcheroo. And yet it gave birth to a masterpiece.

Plotting can never be a cut-and-dried technique—it must always call for utmost creativity. Lloyd Eric Reeve, who teaches magazine-writing at the University of California, told his students: "Our technique of plotting, if it can be dignified by such a term, should probably be called just the 'Technique of Supposing.'" And what is "supposing" but casting our minds hither and thither, forward and backward, in search of alternatives—in search of "what-ifs" and "what-elses"—in search of all kinds of ideas?

Many believe the greatest advertisement ever written was the one Hamilton Watch published under the title: "To Peggy—For Marrying Me in the First Place." This first ran in 1940—was repeated in '41, '48, '49 and '50. It was broadcast, and it was televised. Acclaimed in thousands of letters from the public, it won the highest of all awards.

I happen to know the man who wrote that ad. He agrees that it was his basic idea that made it the hit it was. For days and days, early in 1940, he tried and tried to think up an idea for a Christmas appeal. All-told he wrote down and sketched out over 50 approaches for that one little piece of less than 150 words.

To bag a basic idea like that we have to send our imagination up hill, down dale, and all over the horizon. Although there can be no set technique for this, O. Henry did have a little knack. When he was asked how to write a short story he snapped back, "Just think up the ending and then write your story up to it." But O. Henry was one for putting his imagination on forced draft when need be. One day he simply had to do a story or starve. He thought up the pay-off and then he drove himself into thinking up the whole plot. Thus, within three hours, he created *The Gift of the Magi*.

7.

The material which serves an author best is that which he has gathered along the road of life. W. Somerset Maugham's notebooks occupy 15 thick volumes and cover a period of 57 years. They make no attempt to record his daily doings.

"I meant my notebooks to be a storehouse of materials for future use, and nothing else," he explains. And later: "I have never claimed to create anything out of nothing; I have always needed an incident or a character as a starting point, but I have exercised imagination, invention, and a sense of the dramatic to make it something of my own."

Frank H. Bennett, who began his fiction-writing while teaching music at Nebraska College, says of his files that he built them up by adding one or more ideas each day. "After writing hundreds of yarns over a period of years, I still have something to write about." That, to a writer, is money in the bank!

Bennett points out that ideas abound wherever one happens to be. He urges: "Glance at a newspaper or a magazine, listen to people talk, look at the things about you. Do these, and an inexhaustible horde of ideas will come to you from all sides like showers of meteors. But like meteors, they are fleeting and soon gone if not jotted down."

According to Dale Carnegie, perseverance in writing is what brings out one's creative best. He once spent three years composing three books, and then tossed all his manuscripts into the wastebasket. He devoted more than two years to writing *How to Stop Worrying and Start Living*. He told me, "At the end of six months of effort, that book still didn't march. But I kept painfully on. Finally, the book emerged— after endless rewriting."

In the olden days, when leisure time hung heavier on people's hands, a Dickens or a Thackeray could ignore brevity. But now, with the automobile taking us away from home, and with radio and television taking our time while at home, every writer is called upon to simplify and to condense. "If you have nothing to say, try to say it briefly." That old saw might well be changed to: "No matter how much you have to say, say it in the fewest possible words."

By the way, this book you are reading was first written in three times as many words as now printed. I can testify that my battle against verbosity cost me at least 350 extra hours of creative toil.

John Burroughs pointed out in his *Journals,* "I often think of Lincoln's and Everett's speeches at Gettysburg; one of them has become a classic; of the other not a word has survived in the popular mind." The reasons were that Lincoln's speech sparkled with ideas and that in three minutes he said more than Everett said in two hours—a fact which the latter was kind enough to concede.

8.

If we are to grow creatively, we must gird ourselves against discouragement, a danger that lurks in trying to write for money. We need to use imagination to keep ourselves from giving up too soon.

The odds are mathematically against our selling whatever we may write for publication. We can better our chances by determining where our output is most likely to be wanted.

One way to find out is through the comprehensive guide called *The Writer's Market,* by Ruth A. Jones and Aron M. Mathieu. This sets forth the facts concerning 2500 publications—their editorial requirements, rates of pay, style rules and preferred word lengths. In each case the information is given in the editor's own words.

Ralph H. Major, Jr., an editor of *Coronet,* urges freelancers to "sell the *idea*." He recommends that the contributor first submit an outline of his or her proposed manuscript.

If you can steel yourself against rejection, it is sometimes well to aim high. A little postage will get your manuscript back to you and enable you to send it to a lesser publication. I once submitted to *The Reader's Digest* a piece which was politely turned down. I then sold it to *The Christian Herald*. Four years later the same article was published by a metropolitan newspaper in a full page.

A clash with a taxi driver nettled me into writing an article for *Printers' Ink,* which I knew from long experience would probably pay $25 for it. At the last minute, however, I bravely decided to submit it to *The Reader's Digest* instead. Almost by return mail a check for $1000 fell into my hands.

Over the long run the chances of adequate compensation are so slight that it is better for us semi-pros to make a sideline of our writing, and do it mainly for fun and for creative practice. Samuel Coleridge advised every literary man to keep at some other gainful occupation, and Oliver Wendell Holmes concurred.

Some highly successful authors still stick to their regular jobs. Ed Streeter, who wrote *Dere Mabel* and *The Father of the Bride,* was a pal of mine when we were cub reporters. He early became a banker. And he continued as vice-president of a New York trust company, despite the fact that his writings were in demand and at high prices.

If we use our imagination, rejections need not cause dejection. For one thing, we can put ourselves in the shoes of the greatest authors and realize how they kept going under a barrage of turndowns. W. Somerset Maugham began writing when he was 18; but 10 years elapsed before he could sell enough to make his keep.

Exactly 83 of Ben Ames Williams' manuscripts were rejected during his first four years of literary effort. He kept at his regular job until his manuscripts brought him an adequate income. Since then he has devoted all his working time to writing fiction. "I like to write," he told me. "I like it so well that I've written some 1200 things intended for publication, of which only about 500 have been published."

Many of my friends are desolate over failing to sell their contributions to *The Reader's Digest*. They wouldn't feel so sad if they realized their competition. Some 60 editors constantly comb other publications for material suitable for reprint. Over 30,000 *Digest* readers send in contributions each month.

It's too bad that hardly any of us take rejections as humorously as did Mort Horowitz, who writes for *The Saturday Evening Post*. He once sent a romantic piece to a love magazine, but its lady editor turned him down, saying: "Your stories don't pick me up and swing me along." This struck Horowitz so funny that he shipped her a trapeze.

*   *   *

Let's start writing and keep at it with a well-founded faith that the more we write the better writers we will become— and that through such practice we are sure to develop our creative power in an all-round way.

Chapter 16

CHANGING SHOES can be

a good bending exercise

THE NEXT FEW chapters will deal with human relations —and how we can get along more happily by exercising imagination in such ways as applying the principle laid down in these words: "Therefore all things whatsoever ye would that men should do to you, do ye even so to them."

This golden rule can do most to lessen suffering and to heighten happiness. But, without imagination, it won't work. For we cannot do unto others as we would be done by, unless we mentally put ourselves into their shoes. A *sine qua non* of enlightened selfishness is vicarious imagination.

In frontier days the Omaha Indians taught their young braves this prayer: "Great Spirit, help me never to judge another until I have walked two weeks in his moccasins."

Thus we should change shoes with our fellow humans. But we can even put ourselves into horseshoes, as did Tolstoy. He and Turgenev were walking down a rural lane when they saw an old nag standing alone in the field. Tolstoy crawled through the fence, went over to the horse, put his hand on the animal's neck and spoke to him. Said Turgenev later: "He talked with such sympathy and understanding that Tolstoy at one time must have been a horse."

We can even change shoes with a cow. Ralph Waldo Emerson and his son were trying to push a calf into the barn.

The philosopher shoved the beast from behind; young Emerson pulled her from the front. "Both of us were making the same mistake," said Emerson. "We were thinking only about what we wanted. We forgot what the calf wanted. So the calf stiffened its legs and the more we pushed, the more it resisted."

A witness to that intellectual contest was a young farm girl. She used her imagination. Into the calf's mouth she stuck her finger. The calf sucked it, and willingly let herself be led into the barn.

The fact that changing shoes can flex our creative muscles was recognized by John Erskine: "The body travels more easily than the mind, and until we have limbered up our imagination we continue to think as though we had stayed home. We have not really budged a step until we take up residence in someone else's point of view."

2.

How hard it is to teach teen-agers the wisdom of changing shoes! This was brought home to me one Saturday afternoon while listening to the radio with a boy of 14. The news flashes told of devastating gales all over the East—a hurricane in Florida, a blinding blizzard in Jersey, a tidal wave along the Long Island coast. At mid-afternoon the announcer boomed: "The wires now coming in show that the death toll is already over 100 and still mounting." At this my young friend yelped: "Gee, I wish we could have that storm here!"

But grown-ups likewise lack a sense of other-ness, especially when in a mob. Jim Corbett wrote that after knocking out John L. Sullivan he was disgusted with the crowd: "It struck me as sad to see all those thousands who had given *him* such a wonderful ovation when he entered the ring turning their ovation to me as soon as he was down and out."

One explanation may be that a mob takes its spirit from the least mature among those present—from unthinking adults who have never developed that quality of mind which Harry Overstreet calls "social imagination."

3.

Tact calls for active imagination. One use of it is to break the ice, to put the other fellow at ease—but not quite as Will Rogers once did at the White House. After standing in line at a presidential reception, he finally reached Calvin Coolidge and whispered: "My name is Will Rogers. What's yours?"

Saint Paul in his speech at Mars Hill quickly won his anti-Christian audience by saying that he, too, worshiped an "unknown" God. Time and time again, Christ used superb imagination in making contact with strangers. For example, on the shores of a lake one day He saw two fishermen whom He sought as disciples. They were busy with their nets and talking their trade. To have broken in on them with a plea that they turn to preaching might have invited their snarls.

"Come with me," said Jesus, "and I will make you fishers of men."

"Fishers" was a word that hit home. It helped win them.

Another example was the ice-breaking tact of Mark Twain in his negotiation with General Grant. The ex-president was dying and broke. Twain felt sure he could make a fortune for him if he could persuade him to write his memoirs. The old soldier was frigid until Twain remarked: "General, I'm quite embarrassed. Are you?"

Dr. Norman Vincent Peale tells about his experience as a reporter in a midwest city where he had to gouge news out of a police sergeant. "It was like bearding a lion in his den to talk with him," says Dr. Peale. "I found he had a little grand-daughter, however, and soon realized she was his weakness. One night I surprised him by saying, 'How is that nice little granddaughter of yours?' He melted like snow in the spring-time and became a fast friend." Thus by using imagination we can often turn ice into the milk of kindness.

We can even use imagination to give the other fellow a better time. One afternoon at the Augusta National Golf Club, Ed Dudley, the pro, told me that General Omar Bradley was visiting a nearby Army hospital and would like a game of golf. I lined up two of my friends. None of us knew the General. At dinner that night we figured that he was tired of being asked about war, and veterans, and Russia. So we put ourselves into his boots and conceived a plan of conversation for the next day.

The Chief of Staff joined us at luncheon and we talked of nothing except golf courses we had played. During our 18 holes that afternoon none of us mentioned anything that had to do with his responsibilities. After the game we sat around for an hour and discussed holes-in-one. Each of us, including the General, had at least one entertaining story to tell about such miracles.

Six months later I met General Bradley for the second time in our lives. He immediately remembered me and remarked: "That afternoon we had at Augusta National was certainly a lot of fun."

My brother Russell used his imagination to give waiters a better time. Whereas most of us glue our eyes to our menus and talk over our shoulders at the person serving us, my brother would always turn in his chair, face the waiter, and say: "What would you order if you were I?" Thus he'd put himself into the waiter's shoes, and induce the waiter to put himself into the shoes of the guest. The result? The waiter enjoyed his work the more, and my brother enjoyed better food and cheerier service.

4.

Those are some of the positive ways of using vicarious imagination. Now for a few negatives, mainly by way of foreseeing what *not* to do or say.

Far too many enmities are caused by failure to imagine

how the other fellow will react. For example, in a Chinese city the English colony maintained an ostentatious clubhouse, in the front of which a sign shouted: "No Chinamen or dogs allowed." The newspaperman who told me about that went on to remark: "The white man is through in Asia; it can be largely blamed on that kind of tactlessness."

My partner Bruce Barton is blessed with a deeper sense of sympathy than any man I ever knew. But even he sometimes fails to put himself in the other fellow's shoes—especially if they are golf shoes. Why? Because of over-concentration on his game.

One evening we arrived at a golf course too late to acquire caddies. So we decided to play out of one bag—his bag—with me as the beast of burden.

The course was hilly and the 14 clubs weighed a ton. Coming to the last hole, the steepest grade of all, we were climbing hard when Bruce remarked, "I could have played better if I had had a caddy to tell me what club to use." I just panted and withheld comment. He added, "I wouldn't have looked up so much if I'd had a caddy to watch where my ball was going."

The hill was getting steeper and the bag heavier. At last I spoke up: "I agree with you, Bruce, that it's nice to have a caddy to tell you what club to use, and to watch your ball. but I just thought up *another* reason why it's nice to have a caddy."

"What's that?" asked Bruce.

"To carry your damn golfbag!" I replied with a withering smile.

When we say, "Think twice before you speak," we mean not only to weigh what we are about to say, but also to imagine how our remark will be taken. Most of the discourtesies which cause unhappiness are due to our failure to do that.

According to George Gallup, our nation's three main peeves are: (1) Honking horns in front of houses. (2) Eating

popcorn in movies. (3) Coughing and sneezing in public. All
these annoyances are due to the offenders' failure to put themselves into the shoes of their friends and neighbors.

A clubmate of mine whose plant employs 4000 men was
blocked at an underpass by a traffic jam on a snowy evening
when he was driving home from work. Irked by his long wait,
he started to pull out of line and attempt a detour. A loud
voice stopped him. It was that of one of his own employees
at the wheel of his company's truck. The driver was yelling
at him, "Take it easy, buddy, lots of *overtime* tonight." If
that lad were at all ambitious he might well take on some
shoe-changing exercises.

Harvard University recently made a study of why people
lose their jobs. This showed that only 34 per cent are let out
because of inability to do their work, whereas 66 per cent are
fired for failure in human relations—for inability to put themselves in the other fellow's shoes—for failure to use their
imaginations.

5.

Some derive imaginative exercise from devising practical
jokes; but too seldom do these pranksters foresee the harm
they may do their victims.

Richard J. Peabody has made a study of pranks, both
innocent and pernicious. He favorably cites the case of the
architect who set out to reform his alcoholic friends. As part
of his home, he constructed an "upside down" room, with
flooring nailed to the ceiling and with chairs and tables
fastened to that. Into that delirious chamber, sleeping drunks
were carried; when they awoke, they felt inclined to think
well of the W.C.T.U.

As a despicable example, Mr. Peabody tells about the
"joker" who, during the last World War, published want ads
begging cat owners to turn in their pets at a specified Post
Office—on the plea that mousers were needed to kill rats in

camps of American prisoners in Germany. Over 5000 patriotic cat owners were thus hoaxed.

Isn't it strange that anyone with enough imagination to invent that hocus-pocus would fail to forefeel the pangs of those defrauded cat lovers—would fail to think twice before setting that trap?

6.

A major use of imagination is to see ourselves as others see us. Many a person has run into a dead-end because of failure to do just that. One outstanding case I observed first-hand was that of a man who was blindly obsessed with his own omniscience. By all the logic of seniority he should ulti-mately have headed the great manufacturing company in which he had worked hard for 30 years. But he was passed over when the president died, and an outsider was hired instead.

"Have you ever seen a man throw his weight around and try to make you feel small?" asked Henry J. Taylor. "If so, don't get angry. Pity that person. He has no imagination." Taylor cited a minor executive who, when promoted, promptly developed a big head. When his associates sensed this, they no longer tried to help him. His progress was stopped.

Most of our "boy wonders" rise to the heights too soon, get dizzy, and fall back. Adulation blinds them so that they fail to see themselves as others see them. On the other hand, "slow burners" who plod through their early years and blossom at mid-life—they have to watch their step all the way. They form the habit of seeing themselves in a truer light, and of putting themselves into the shoes of all with whom they work.

Women readers won't like this, but they might ask them-selves: "Do I see myself as others see me or only as my mirror shows me?" For instance, do girls who pile on too much lipstick ever wonder how they look to men? That's a mild hint compared to Robert Ruark's tirade:

"Each year, when the mistletoe season sneaks closer, I find somehow that the old man's heart isn't in it. Time was when you could snatch a bundle of dry goods up in your arms, plaster your lips on hers, and feel mildly exhilarated, as though you had just snatched a kiss from a woman. No more. Any time I purloin a peck in a dark parlor, I am kissing no woman. I feel I am kissing Batten, Barton, Durstine & Osborn. . . . It kills my romantic yen to think that I am going to chew through a half inch of Cherry, Cinnamon Stick, Barberry, Apple Red, Turkey Red, Raspberry, Pimento or Red Burgundy."

          ❖   ❖   ❖

There's hardly a waking minute when we are not called upon to use imagination vicariously. By constantly trying to change shoes we can grow creatively. But for a more active exercise—instead of passively applying the golden rule—we might make ourselves "go over to the other side," as the next chapter will explain.

Chapter 17

"CASTING BREAD" can flex

our creative sinews

B<small>Y</small> PUTTING THE golden rule into *action*, we practice what psychology calls *empathy*—"the imaginative projection of one's own consciousness into another being." This should call for thinking up things to do for the other fellow and *doing* them, thus bringing into play not merely vicarious imagination but also creativity.

Even tying the other fellow's shoelace can be good exercise. And such services can be fun, as Fred B. Barton continually proved. Before visiting a friend's home he would think up some little favor to perform while there. On an overnight stay at our house—with his own screwdriver and can of oil—he put to right about a dozen of our squeaky and wobbly doorknobs and locks. Another friend, Fred Waring, heals so many little ills that he is known as "Doc." His specialty is removing cinders from eyes—an operation he performs with a handkerchief and matchstick.

Such trivia, of course, serve merely to make our relations more pleasant. When applied to more serious ends, however, little acts empowered by empathy and persistently carried on can almost move mountains—as James Keller proved in his book about the Christophers, *You Can Change the World.*

2.

David Dunn, in *Try Giving Yourself Away*, quotes a New Englander as saying: "It takes courage to give a small portion of yourself in lieu of some obviously valuable article. But a lively imagination made it possible for me to perceive a great many ways in which I might 'spend myself,' instead of the cash I lacked."

Dunn points out how such *spending* usually turns out to be *investing—"provided you give away with no thought of reward."* Nor should we expect immediate dividends. "Cast thy bread upon the waters; for thou shalt find it after many days." And this often means many months or even years.

As I look back over my own life, I can testify that almost every good break in my career came from trying to tie someone else's shoelace. Oh, how I wish I could convince young cynics that he who serves unselfishly gets further in the long run. The healthier our imagination, the surer we are to sense this truth.

3.

Courtesy can be a vacuous thank-you or a conscious course of action. My friend Harry Lehman, head of a large company, advocated "Courtesy Always." He continually urged his supervisors to give a helping hand to new workers, to welcome back warmly those who have been away and ill, to extend hearty congratulations for jobs well done.

"No matter how busy we are, we owe it to ourselves and to those with whom we work to make certain that courtesy is a *first* order of business at all times." This was Harry's creed, and he personally practiced it with all his might.

Ben Duffy, who went from office boy to president of a big company, was another exemplar. He insisted that his associates show the same courtesy to salesmen and job-seekers as to paying clients. He believed, as Emerson did, that "Life is not so short but that there is always time for courtesy."

A large store recently put on an employee contest with television sets as prizes for courtesy, the customers electing the winners. This did much to inspire the store's staff to think creatively on how to "pass over unto" the other side of the counter.

Why not conduct a contest for customers, with the store's employees as the judges? There is certainly room for more courtesy on the part of the public toward salespeople. Recent surveys have shown up the three main ways in which we shoppers act boorishly: (1) We fail to express appreciation for extra effort. (2) We take our personal peeves out on the salespeople. (3) We insist on being waited upon out of turn.

My youngest daughter recently made me feel proud. She knitted a sweater, and turned it over to a woman for blocking—a woman who worked all day and, for added income, blocked sweaters at night. My teen-ager not only paid her regular charge, but wrote a note of appreciation. That woman talked of that act of courtesy for weeks and weeks.

Active courtesy, even when conventional, can help keep our imaginations aglow. But to think up extra and unusual ways to express appreciation—that can be creative exercise of a high order.

4.

Said George Matthew Adams: "He who praises another enriches himself far more than he enriches the one praised." And from the standpoint of creative exercise, when we go out of the way to praise—when we try to think up surprising ways to do so—we help tone up our imaginative muscles.

If bosses would only put on their subordinates' shoes, they would be more inclined toward laudation. Thank heavens, some companies believe in this to the point of systematically slapping associates on the back. My hat is off to General Mills and its Vice-president Samuel Gale, who officially pinned a rose on some member of his staff almost every day.

If we parents want to develop creative power in our children, we should seek opportunities to praise them for whatever they do along creative lines. In my case, I still recall how, as a little boy, my father inspired me by raving about a gadget I had invented and had tried to make with my own hands.

But it's not too easy to praise, as Dorothy Blake pointed out: "We often seem so self-conscious and fearful in expressing words of praise or affection—so afraid that we might be called sentimental or gushing—that we hold in tight reserve the pieces of our minds that could do a world of good in human relations."

While walking home one evening, I was fascinated by a window display in a flower shop. So I went in and asked who had created that gem. The florist pointed to a young man at work potting plants. I went over to him and said: "Wow! that's a wonderful window. I understand that you did it. I stopped in to congratulate you." He glared at me. He seemed sure I was trying to sell him a brass brick. I felt like turning on my heel, but I stopped and finally convinced him of my sincerity.

A slap in the face in exchange for a slap on the back is such a rare exception that it should not discourage us. What we really ought to do would be to give ourselves a daily stint of thinking up something to praise, and in some unexpected way. Just trying to hit upon such an idea every day would be good creative practice.

5.

Christmas is a training season for the game of thinking up. To choose the right gifts, we not only must change shoes with those to whom we give, but must conjure up countless alternatives.

Let's try to think up something surprisingly unexpected as well as pat, as did Mrs. Harry Payne when choosing a Christmas present for her husband. She knew that, with all his abilities, he lacked self-confidence. So her gift to Harry was a course in public speaking.

Instead of presenting that to him in a conventional way, she arranged that on Christmas morning Harry would find among his presents a personal letter from Dale Carnegie, announcing that Mrs. Payne had bought the course for him. Dale's pen-written postscript said: "I will look forward to seeing you on January 11."

That it is not the *money* but the *imagination* which makes a gift is especially true when it comes to our little ones. I know of one tot who, on Christmas morning, received a $100 train, including a locomotive with a bell that rang and a stack that smoked. He passed that by and dashed avidly toward two other gifts he had espied under the tree—a make-believe electric razor and a mechanical grasshopper that cost a quarter.

Another five-year-old child, deep in expensive gifts on Christmas morning, gleefully opened one after another to the delight of his doting parents. Suddenly he stopped, looked up at his dad and asked, "What happened to that rubber ball on a string I got for my birthday? I want that."

Shopping calls for judgment—and imagination. An extreme case in point was confessed to me by my friend George Eager, promotion manager of *The Bulletin* in Philadelphia. One Christmas he sought a suit of pajamas for his wife. Pressed for time, he went to Wanamaker's, only to find the store too packed with women for him to get attention. So he thought up a crazy stunt. He whispered to a saleswoman, "I want your help in picking out a suit of pajamas for a beautiful girl—*not* for my wife." That whisper turned the trick.

When we make our own Christmas gifts, we exercise imagination far more than when we buy them. Mrs. Esther de Forest told me that the presents which she and her children give to some 20 people every year are designed by her and hand-made in every case. What a creative hothouse her home must be!

Thinking up tokens to take the place of gifts can likewise tax imagination. Short of cash one year, Ernestine Evans conceived the plan of giving I.O.U.'s for Christmas. One note promised "one party" to a couple who lived in a hotel. To a friend still in Vassar her I.O.U. read: "Do you want my flat for a week end in February? You can bring three of your friends. I shall be away, and the refrigerator will be full."

A 12-year-old boy in our neighborhood has been saving up for a man-size sailboat. He needs about $1000 more. His seven-year-old brother pondered this problem last Christmas. All on his own he thought up an appropriate gift—a rope, with which his big brother could tie his yacht to the dock. This is the kind of ingenuity that makes a creative calisthenic out of Christmas.

Even municipalities can think up little gifts surprising enough to make them seem big. During the week before Christmas, those who violated the parking laws of East Orange, New Jersey, received a greeting instead of a police ticket—a cordial note saying that the patrolman on duty had inserted a nickel in the parking meter. The message ended: "Come always to East Orange. Merry Christmas."

6.

How about gifts at other times? How about stretching our imaginations to put surprise into them? How about a new twist in timing, for instance?

Lieutenant Guy Hairston, Jr., had completed 106 jet missions over Korea—had won nine medals for bravery. He had hoped to be home by Christmas, but he arrived on February 10. He came to a house decorated with holly and mistletoe—into a living room radiant with a lighted Christmas tree. While his father and mother looked on, he sat on the floor beside a mechanical Santa Claus which played *Jingle Bells*, and opened his "Christmas" gifts. After the flier returned to Korea, a reporter asked his parents what their neighbors thought about their changing the date of Christmas. "Everyone thought we were crazy," the Hairstons laughed. "But *he* liked it."

Even gifts of flowers can be timed imaginatively. My friend Birge Kinne sends flowers *after* a funeral—usually on a Sunday, a week or so later. I saw a note the widow of an old pal sent to him:

"You know, of course, that Joe was buried last Wednesday. Today is Sunday and it is my toughest day. I couldn't imagine who was ringing the doorbell this morning. It turned out to be the florist's son, with that lovely bouquet from you. I went to church. It was terrible to sit in our pew without Joe. When I came back I dreaded coming into the house, but I made it—and what a difference it meant to have those two dozen roses of yours smiling at me from the top of our piano."

Going-away presents are likewise a challenge to imagination. My daughter Joan and her husband were about to drive their young children from Buffalo to Tennessee to show them to their grandmother. As they pulled out of their garage that morning, Mrs. William Oliver stopped them and gave them a big paper bag containing 12 packages—one to be opened each morning for the four-year-old, and one to be opened each morning for the two-year-old, while en route. Can you imagine anything else that could have meant so much to that mother on that trip?

When we fail to put imagination into our gifts, we can fall flat on our faces, as I did some years ago when a young woman on our staff became engaged to a wealthy client of ours. Thinking of what my own daughters might like, I bought her an electric sewing machine. "You ought to know," she angrily told me, "that I have been making my own living and my own dresses all my life, and that when I get married I will never sew another stitch. The last thing I want is a sewing machine."

In contrast, I cite a Japanese whom General MacArthur and many others regarded as the "Grand Old Man of Japan," Aisaku Hayashi by name. A Christian, he wanted his race to emulate Americans. So when my last book came out, he spent 12 months translating it for his people.

A year later I dined at the home of J. P. McEvoy, who had just returned from Japan, and he handed me a package he had brought from Tokyo—a present for me from Mr. Hayashi. And what a present!—a kakemono. With it, a longhand letter explained: "Please accept this with my best wishes as a memento from my country. This hanging scroll was painted for me in 1910 by Koson Mochizuki. Chinese writing on the side may roughly be rendered: 'Day's Long Mountains Peaceful.'"

Even continuing programs of giving can be thought up. Mrs. Walter Monday of Mt. Washington, Ohio, worked up a gift exchange. Here's her story: "A friend and I live a great distance from each other. As we have been friends from childhood, we are familiar with each other's tastes; so we each keep a 'special gift' shopping bag, with the other's name labeled on it, hanging in our respective closets. Into this bag go recipes the other might like, toys, pieces of clothing outgrown by one's own children but suitable for the other's, premium coupons the other is saving, new pieces to be added to the other's hobby collections, magazines with articles of particular interest. Thus periodically we exchange shopping bags as eagerly as children exchange gifts on Christmas."

It has been my good luck to be the recipient of surprises on my birthday. Each year, for 30 years, I received from Alexander Woollcott on May 24 an out-of-the-ordinary greeting. The one I remember best was a cable he sent me from China, saying: "I am the only elephant in Asia who never forgets."

Another friend who comes through with an idea each year to enliven my birthday is Girard Hammond. With a surprisingly appropriate present, he always includes a note on the stationery of a company for which we both worked in 1926—a firm whose name was changed in 1928. I hope I live long enough for him to use up on me the stock of obsolete letterheads he has hoarded.

7.

The ultimate in shoe-changing calls for taking ourselves out of our well-heeled shoes and putting ourselves into the broken shoes of the less fortunate. This calls for the utmost in empathy.

Charity means love rather than handouts. Free doughnuts and coffee were not what built the Salvation Army into the hearts of millions. Its real appeal has been its feeling for the underdog, as summed up in the slogan coined by Bruce Barton: "A man may be down but never out."

Putting oneself into the shoes of the less fortunate is the secret of Alcoholics Anonymous. What a shining example of altruism this organization is—and what a tribute to man's power of imagination.

Over the years, all the medicines, religions, and "cures" had succeeded in rehabilitating less than four per cent of the alcoholics. But, by changing places with other victims, A.A. members are putting on their feet for good about 50 per cent of those who seek their help.

To drop a dime into a blind man's cup calls for far less imagination than to pay something toward the support of an institution which is helping blind people in real ways, such as teaching them new trades. When asked to give to that Blind Institute, not directly, but through our Community Chest, we need to think even more creatively—to foresee what would happen to all the chest-financed causes if we all failed to do our part—to foresee the chaos which might come to our community if it had no federated fund, and if every cause campaigned for its own financial needs.

Personal excursions in do-goodery can sometimes fall flat for lack of facts to guide us—as Clarence Davis and I found out one Christmas many years ago. Led solely by impulse, we delivered a huge basket of fruit to the home of a woman who was rumored to be in want. We rang the doorbell. She opened the door. We sweetly told her of our mission. She angrily told us off, and slammed the door in our faces.

Some personal benevolences, however, can be quite sound. One such was thought up by a schoolteacher, Mrs. Muriel Soulé. Her new plan started with Cyril, a seemingly bright pupil, but listless. Mrs. Soulé found the facts: His mother was a widow and worked nights as a telephone operator. The boy took care of his brother of six and his sister of four.

Cyril's overcoat was threadbare. Mrs. Soulé told him: "Ask your mother if she would let me give you a warmer coat. Explain to her that as a teacher I have friends whose boys have outgrown their clothes." A grateful "yes" came back to Mrs. Soulé; and thus she set herself up as a one-woman clothing exchange—not only for the needy boys and girls in her class, but for their little brothers and sisters as well.

* * *

It's relatively easy for any of us to put ourselves into others' shoes, or even to practice empathy. The extent to which we do so depends upon our intelligence, upon our will, and upon a somewhat simple use of imagination by way of thinking up what-elses, how-elses and other such alternatives.

Being about to consider tougher creative tasks, let us now scan the mental procedure applicable to *problems*—problems which require a more thorough search for solutions.

Chapter 18

PROBLEM SOLVING—

the best of all creative exercises

SINCE THE NEXT few chapters will deal with problems, at home and on the job, let's now consider how creativity works when thoroughly applied.

Although physical facts are easier to nail down than psychic facts, nobody yet knows *exactly* how babies are born. No wonder, then, that we are still at sea as to exactly how ideas are born. Perhaps neither of these mystic processes will ever be fully comprehended.

About 50 years ago, Henri Poincaré set forth the mental processes of mathematical creation. He could do that quite precisely, compared to what anyone can do in regard to non-mathematical problems—for the reason that Poincaré dealt with elements which were tangible and constant, rather than intangible and variable.

The more I study and practice creativity, the surer I feel that its process is necessarily a stop-and-go, a catch-as-catch-can, a ring-around-the-rosie; and the more I doubt whether it can ever be "exact" enough to rate as scientific. The most we can honestly say is that it usually includes some or all of these phases:

1. *Orientation:* Picking out and pointing up the problem.

2. *Preparation:* Gathering material relevant to the problem.

3. *Analysis:* Breaking down the relevant material.

4. *Hypothesis:* Piling up alternatives by way of tentative ideas.

5. *Incubation:* Letting up in order to invite illumination.

6. *Synthesis:* Putting the pieces together.

7. *Verification:* Judging the resultant ideas.

In actual practice, we can follow no such one-two-three sequence. We may start our guessing even while preparing. Analysis may lead us straight to the solution. After incubation, we may again go digging for facts which, at the start, we did not know we needed. And, of course, we might bring verification to bear on our hypotheses, thus to cull our "wild stabs" and proceed with only the likeliest.

All along the way we must change pace. We push and then coast, and then push. By driving our conscious minds in search of additional facts and hypotheses, we develop a psychic force—a concentration of thought and feeling strong enough to accelerate our automatic pump of association, and make it well up still more ideas. Thus through strenuous effort we indirectly induce "idle" illumination.

The ideal mind is that which can create as well as evaluate—can even judge its own brain-children. Criticism goes with idea-production, but only if kept in its place. If premature, it tends to deaden our creative drive. By and large, judgment should be stalled until we reach the stage of verification.

2.

Preparation, normally the first step in a creative process, calls for two kinds of knowledge—that which we have previously stored and that which we gather anew to bear upon our creative problem.

Memory serves as a supply tank. The octane of its fuel depends on how we have taken it in. Whatever we have gained by active striving and firsthand experience is far richer than that which we store through idle spectating, listless reading, and empty chatter.

It takes imagination to think up just what new knowledge to seek; and we can often guide our research better if we first think up hypotheses. Moreover, in our very digging for data we often unearth ideas.

Then, of course, we should *analyze* our relevant material. And in picking our data to pieces we should look for factors of similarity, for these may reveal a pattern and lead us to a framework.

We must also analyze the problem itself. As Charles F. Kettering explained, "The process of research is to pull the problem apart into its different elements, a great many of which you already know about. When you get it pulled apart, you can work on the things you don't know about."

Questions can be keys to the right kind of analysis. For instance, if asked to dream up a new outside sign for our church, we might start by writing down headings like these: Purpose? Location? Design? Material? Illumination? Lettering? Erection? Under each of these we might spell out subquestions. For example as to purpose, should it be: 1. To remind parishioners of services? 2. To attract visitors? 3. To build goodwill?

All told we would thus list about 30 points which would clarify our objective, indicate data to be sought, and help us get further faster with our creative thinking.

More complex problems should be broken down into their components in order that we may aim at simpler targets. For example: If upset over her husband's morals, a wife would face the basic problem of "How can I make him a better man?" But that covers too much ground for creative attack. She might better start by making a list of influences which corrupt him, and another list of influences which might reform him. She could then single out her targets, such as: "How can I get him to attend church with me?"

According to Warren W. Coxe, New York State's Director of Educational Research, "We need far more work on analysis of problems than on collection of data. We need not only to analyze the problems, but to arrive at some hypothesis as to what the solution may be, even before we gather our data."

3.

When piling up hypotheses, we should go the limit. Obviously, the more ideas we accumulate, the better our chance of hitting upon the right ones. Quantity may thus insure quality, as was brought out by Dr. J. P. Guilford, President of the American Psychological Association: "The person who is capable of producing a large number of ideas per unit of time, other things being equal, has a greater chance of having significant ideas."

By asking ourselves "else" questions we can pile up quantities of ore by way of hypotheses, out of which we can refine gold in the form of solutions. "*What*-else," "*where*-else," "*when*-else," "*how*-else," "*who*-else," "*why*-else"—all these "elses" are helpful. And so are the "what-ifs." By foreseeing contingencies, we can add to our "elses."

When we hunt hypotheses we should ride our minds afar —a fact illustrated by an experience related to me by a New York doctor of high standing. As a young practitioner, he treated a patient for yellow jaundice over a period of three years. He failed—not through lack of medical knowledge but through paucity of hypotheses. He overlooked the possibility that his patient might be a Chinese, which, in fact, was what he turned out to be.

Here are a few guides to the kinds of self-interrogation which can lead to ideas:

Put to other uses? New ways to use as is? Other uses if modified?

Adapt? What else is like this? What other idea does this suggest? Does past offer parallel? What could I copy? Whom could I emulate?

Modify? New twist? Change meaning, color, motion, sound, odor, form, shape? Other changes?

Magnify? What to add? More time? Greater frequency? Stronger? Higher? Longer? Thicker? Extra value? Plus ingredient? Duplicate? Multiply? Exaggerate?

Minify? What to subtract? Smaller? Condensed? Miniature? Lower? Shorter? Lighter? Omit? Streamline? Split up? Understate?

Substitute? Who else instead? What else instead? Other ingredient? Other material? Other process? Other power? Other place? Other approach? Other tone of voice?

Re-arrange? Interchange components? Other pattern? Other layout? Other sequence? Transpose cause and effect? Change pace? Change schedule?

Reverse? Transpose positive and negative? How about opposites? Turn it backward? Turn it upside down? Reverse roles? Change shoes? Turn tables? Turn other cheek?

Combine? How about a blend, an alloy, an assortment, an ensemble? Combine units? Combine purposes? Combine appeals? Combine ideas?

Quite a few people now use that list for priming their mental pumps. A manufacturer privately printed 375 copies for his supervisory associates to keep on top of their desks. Bonnie Driscoll told me how she had applied that same self-quiz:

"About to produce a Fashion Show at the Waldorf Astoria, I tried in vain for nearly a month to line up the needed ideas. Then I started to ask myself that list of questions. Within two hours I had 28 ideas—28 in two hours after three weeks of no ideas at all."

It goes without saying that hunting for hypotheses is an exercise which can do much to make us more creative.

4.

To open our minds to stray ideas we occasionally ease up and make way for that phase of the creative process which is known as incubation, the mystic quality of which has impressed many authors. Some of them refer to it as "illumination," others as "inspiration." E. D. Hutchinson described it as "the phenomenon of insight." Theodor Reik called it "listening with the third ear." Don Herold dubbed it "the fine art of beneficial floating."

Henry James made much of the "deep well of unconscious cerebration." Emerson took time out each day for "meditating quietly before brooks." Shakespeare called incubation "the spell in which imagination bodies forth the forms of things unknown." Somerset Maugham wrote, "Reverie is the groundwork of creative imagination."

Even science recognizes the value of incubation's flashes. Dr. Walter B. Cannon of Harvard, after 40 years in physiological research, wrote in his book entitled *The Role of Hunches:* "From the years of my youth, the unearned assistance of sudden and unpredicted insight has been common." He investigated the creative habits of 232 high-standing chemists and found that over a third of them gave credit to hunches.

The mystery of incubation is partly explained by our power of association, which automatically links words or ideas with other words or ideas. Ancient Greece gave us the three laws which govern this phenomenon: contiguity, similarity, and contrast.

We should allow plenty of time for incubation, and should let ourselves loose—even playfully so. In describing his periods of illumination, Mark Twain wrote: "I use the meridians of longitude and parallels of latitude for a seine, and drag the Atlantic Ocean for whales. I scratch my head with the lightning and purr myself to sleep with the thunder."

At other times, however, we might purposely run our reveries. Tom Dreier, conservative New Englander, once told me: "Before going to see a prospect I have sat in a chair and imagined my way through the sales problem from the first contact to a successful finish." Guided imagining thus helped him win clients.

As the story goes, Raphael, employed to paint a picture on a chapel wall, annoyed the monks of the monastery by idling for three whole days, just gazing at the blank space. But Raphael knew that such "lolling" helped him open the windows of his mind for what Masefield later called "butterflies," a term for stray ideas.

Beardsley Ruml, the "national idea man," locked himself up for at least an hour a day and did nothing but muse. He described this kind of brown study as "a state of dispersed attention." Incidentally, he ardently believed in man's ability to turn on his creative faucet at will. While a professor at Chicago University, he once challenged President Robert Hutchins with: "If you can't give me a new idea in the next 15 minutes, you're fired."

Even inspiration can be courted, and one way to do this is to take a walk. Since the days of Thoreau, hiking has often helped to woo ideas.

After a Thanksgiving dinner at the home of my daughter in Syracuse, I took a stroll in the rain. The community struck me as a cross-section of America. Out of that thought came the idea of establishing a consumer-research panel of 1000 families in that city, an insignificant inspiration which turned out to be a fruitful idea for my company.

We can even let our imagination work while motoring. So hopeful am I that good ideas may come floating through my car windows, I drive with a yellow pad alongside me. Perhaps I should be arrested for this; but the reverse happened on my way home one evening.

A cop barked: "Pull over!"

"You've got me!" I winced. "My only excuse for passing that stop sign is that I was talking to Tommy Loughran at the time."

"Don't try to kid me! You're *alone*. What do you mean, you were talking to our old light-heavyweight champion?"

I explained: "Last night I went with him to a studio where he had a spot on television. Just as I was turning that corner I was telling Tommy about an idea I had just cooked up for a half-hour show of his own."

The officer believed me. Tommy was an old hero of his. So off I went scot-free.

Sleep often helps us to hatch out ideas. Jack Lacy, nationally known sales trainer, told me that just before his bedtime he concentrates on something he has been trying to work out during the day. "By doing this, I often find myself waking up in the night with some clear and good ideas."

"Soak!" That's Don Herold's prescription for creative incubation. He claims that we can never think up as well in showers as in tubs. Joseph Conrad habitually took to his bath for his spells of illumination. On the other hand, Shelley found that by floating paper boats in his tub he could best court his muse.

Shaving is a proverbial inducer of ideas. Composer Brahms, however, claimed that his best musical flashes came to him while shining his shoes.

Whitney Williams made a study of what Hollywood writers do for inspiration. Script-writer Herbert Baker turns to the piano and improvises while waiting for new ideas to come his way. Dorothy Kingsley meditates in a church across the street from her studio. Mildred Gordon, who co-authors with her husband, woos her muse by going out and buying a new hat. "Her spouse sometimes figures it would be cheaper if she were to abandon writing entirely, since she rapidly is building up a chapeau inventory which makes Hedda Hopper's pale into insignificance," Whitney Williams wrote.

Edward Streeter believes that incubation needs nudging. He told me: "The stream of ideas flows continuously during all our waking hours, and along this stream priceless ideas are passing. The thing to do is to try to catch them as they go by. We should make a rough note of every idea just as soon as it occurs to us, regardless of where we are. Somehow or other the very doing of this seems to stimulate kindred ideas."

A most ingenious method of memo-making is used by a New York lawyer. He always carries a pack of government postcards, addressed to himself. Whenever an idea hits him—whether on the subway or in the bathroom—he jots it down on one of the cards and sticks it in the mail.

As to other phases of the creative process, synthesis puts together the pieces of the puzzle. If we prepare adequately, set our aim correctly, and marshall enough hypotheses, synthesis may come at any stage—even during incubation.

Verification calls for realism. As Luigi Galvani warned, "It is easy to deceive oneself into believing that he has found just that which he had set out to discover."

When applying our own judgment we might well analyze our solution by setting down on paper all of its pros and cons. And, of course, we should also enlist the judgment of others. The surest method of verification, however, is to put our ideas to test. And to think up the best way to test is a creative exercise of itself.

5.

The creative process calls for intellectual effort, or emotional drive, or both. When impassioned by hunger, fear, hate or love, our fervor is self-starting and automatic. Normally, however, we must gird our creativity with determination.

Writers recognize as "rhythms of creativity" the ups and downs of their power to produce. Since each person's talent is the same from day to day, those cycles must be solely cycles of energy—a fact which helps prove how dependent upon our drive our creativity can be.

Effort even has its place in association of ideas, according to Dorothy Sayers. She put these words into the mouth of her Lord Peter Wimsey: "If ever you want to commit a murder, the thing you've got to do is prevent people from associatin' their ideas. Most people don't associate anythin'—their ideas just roll about like so many dry peas on a tray, makin' a lot of noise and goin' nowhere; but once you begin lettin' 'em string their peas into a necklace, it's goin' to be strong enough to hang you, what?"

That kind of stringing together is what Graham Wallas hailed as "correlation." This calls for scanning the little ideas which well up into our minds and scrutinizing them for likenesses. By such conscious thinking we can supplement the automatic power of our associationism.

The wife of a lawyer friend of mine was prone to nag him for just sitting and thinking during the evening. "Why don't you *do* something?" was her wail. After he had won his most lucrative case, he gently chided her: "I hope you can understand now that when I am sitting here of an evening, and seem to be daydreaming, I am really doing my hardest and most profitable work."

To run our reveries instead of letting our reveries run us is not so easy, as an authoress I know found out: "I once tried to keep track of the things my mind touched upon when left to its own devices while I ironed one shirt. I lost count. My mind roamed like a drunkard and got nowhere. I have to lasso, hog-tie, and sit on my thought-processes to get anything out of my mental meandering. I believe that exercises in imagination should include exercises in concentration itself."

Said Emerson: "The hardest task in the world is to think." Jefferson Machamer went further in a cartoon of his which showed one teen-ager saying to another, "I bet I waste two or three hours a day just *thinking*, and I'm going to cut it out."

A Swiss meticulously recorded his 80 years, and calculated that he had spent 26 years in bed, and 21 years at labor. Eating took him six years. He was angry nearly six years. He wasted more than five years waiting for tardy people. Shaving occupied 228 days, scolding his children took 26 days, tying his neckties 18 days, blowing his nose 13 days, lighting his pipe 12 days. He laughed for only 46 hours in all his life. He recorded no time spent on *thinking*, in all those 80 years.

General Lauris Norstad is rated by many as the creative brain of our Air Force. Justice Felix Frankfurter chided him:

"You are just another executive. If you were a success you would devote only three or four hours a day to being an executive and the rest of the time to *thinking*."

A simple device by which to get going creatively is to set a time and place. My author friends tell me that they find it best to collar themselves at a set hour each day and chain themselves to their typewriters.

But we need a pay-off as well as a date. So, let's set dead-lines. Let's give I.O.U.'s. By committing ourselves in that way we tend to add emotional drive to our creative effort.

Quotas can also help us stretch our imaginations. Suppose we set ourselves a stint of only 10 ideas. Having thought those up, we are apt to find ourselves in stride, and likely to run on to many more ideas. We can nudge that kind of momentum by using a pair of wonderful gadgets, commonly known as pencil and pad.

6.

Another way to induce creative drive is to team up. Collaboration tends to keep us on our imaginative toes, and also to spur our automatic power of association. On this latter point, Thomas Carlyle said: "The lightning-spark of thought, generated in the solitary mind, awakens its likeness in another mind." This contagion between mentalities has been called "chain reaction" by Dr. Albert Butzer.

Yes, two heads are better than one for creative thinking. Many of our most brilliant discoveries have come from married couples working together, and from the teaming up of men with men, and women with women.

One of the shortcomings of business is its failure to take advantage of the fact that even groups can think creatively. Although nearly every company has conferences galore, most of these sessions put a premium on judicial thinking, and accordingly penalize creative thinking.

Strictly creative conferences have proved highly productive in countless cases. In such brainstorming huddles a problem is posed, and all present are urged to come up with ideas for its solution—nothing but ideas, even the zaniest. The only thing barred is *criticism*. Verification is deferred until *after* imagination has had its full fling.

A bridge group or church group might well devote an occasional evening to that kind of idea practice. David Beetle is president of an outing club. He and his fellow officers had always thought up the plans for excursions. "This year," he told me, "we sliced up our membership into 10 committees, and got each group to think up ideas. This has worked out swell. We have more and better plans than ever before. And what fun these 10 committees have had—not to mention the good they got out of limbering up their imaginations."

A girls' school, about to celebrate its centennial, selected my wife to head a planning committee. She invited its members to lunch and asked them to spend an hour thinking up together. They developed over 100 ideas. That evening, two of the women 'phoned Mrs. Osborn to report still other suggestions.

Mrs. Colin Douglas, of New York City, has started a "Fatties Anonymous." Under her leadership, groups of people weighing upward of 200 have been organized to discuss causes of obesity, and to think up ways to reduce.

A Chicago lawyer named Samuel Starr, veteran of over 3000 divorce cases, has established "Divorcees Anonymous" —a panel of divorcees brought together to think with him on how to steer couples away from marital rocks. These 100 conferees, because of their own experience, can often suggest workable plans for reconciliation before too late. According to the *Chicago Daily News*, this creative clinic has been salvaging marriages at the rate of more than one a day.

Those women are doing something for their troubled sisters, and at the same time building up their minds. By thinking creatively in a group, they vigorously exercise their imaginations.

7.

Since creative thinking calls for emotional drive, it should be kept free from emotional blocks such as timidity. This handicap sometimes stems from false dignity—the fear of looking *foolish*. More often its cause is honest skepticism as to one's ability to think up anything worth while. Here is where we should heed Shakespeare's warning: "Our doubts are traitors, and make us lose the good we oft might win, by fearing to attempt."

Akin to timidity is failure-phobia—the dread of venturing and *losing*. In the arena of ideas, we have to laugh off our knockdowns—we have to turn our knockouts into comebacks.

Another block is perfectionism—a virtue which when carried to excess can hamstring imagination. All of us have to beware of this because creative energies thrive on self-encouragement and whatever we do to discourage ourselves blights our creativity by killing our effort.

What positive things can we do to condition ourselves creatively? First of all, let's open our minds, let's make ourselves mentally outreaching. Let's encourage our curiosity and even try to activate it to the limit.

And let's cultivate audacity as well as curiosity. Let's steel ourselves to risk ridicule. Said Robert Louis Stevenson, "Give me the young man who has brains enough to make a fool of himself."

Professional inventor Dr. C. W. Fuller recommends hitching one's imagination to a star. "Enthusiasm," said he, "is the fuel which fires the imagination; and enthusiasm rises highest when we make the sky the limit. We should let our imagination run riot—then gradually harness it to an idea which seems worthwhile, working from the general to the specific. In this way, creative thinking becomes fascinating—and develops a pleasant habit which grows and grows with use."

Chapter 19

MARITAL PROBLEMS—

let's tackle them creatively

MARRIAGE IS a creative challenge. As Ian Maclaren pointed out, "we sin against our dearest, not because we do not love, but because we do not *imagine*."

America's marital record shows that two out of three matings last a lifetime. On the other hand, Dr. Clifford R. Adams made a 10-year study and found that only 17 per cent of married people are really happy with each other. The contentment of the other 83 per cent could certainly be improved by more creative thinking.

Two people dear to me wrecked their lives through failure to put themselves into each other's shoes. When the husband was stricken with arthritis, the exuberantly healthy wife let her imagination lapse to the point where she even ridiculed his sufferings.

Years later the divorced husband told me: "After a night of agony I arose one morning to find that I could not stand on my feet. I was sitting on my bed, painfully trying to pull on my shoes when she came into my room. She laughed at my plight. That *tore* it!"

"Kiss-and-make-up" may work fine at first but often later runs up against the law of diminishing returns. A far better rule is to kiss and *think* up—think up ways of *avoiding* the clashes which would otherwise call for making up. That kind

179

of imaginative exercise helps us not only to safeguard our happiness, but also to build up our minds.

2.

A recent song-hit, "Use Your Imagination," features the theme: "Every day will be a perfect dream," meaning marriage. Such sophistry misguides many boys and girls who, having observed their own parents, *should know* that marriage can never be all nectar and caviar. If our youngsters used their imaginations, they would project that knowledge into a truer picture of what their own marriage would be like.

One of the fallacies was recently pointed out by psychologist Laurence Gould: "The idea that there is just *one* 'right person' for you is romantic nonsense. Its actual basis is childish." Robertson Davies added: "Love, like ice cream, is a beautiful thing, but nobody should regard it as adequate provision for a long and adventurous journey."

The first year is fraught with danger. During courtship we warp our imaginations—we see each other through rose-colored glasses. Then we start living together and realism sets in. Said marriage counselor Jacques Bacal: "I wish every newly married couple could realize that conflict during the first year of marriage is the rule, not the exception."

Another authority on marriage, Dr. David R. Mace, has urged: "We must kill the lie that marriage is a kind of emotional Turkish bath in which two people recline in blissful ease and let the world go by. Marriage does offer the joys and fulfillments we yearn for, but these come as the reward of work." And what is meant by "work"? What else could it mean except working our minds creatively to keep clear of the rocks which threaten every marital cruise? And such thinking calls for effort. Every bride and groom should know, in advance, this truth as set down by E. H. Young: "Loving people is easy—but living with them isn't."

All thinkers will agree with Dr. Clifford R. Adams that couples need more briefing before they near the altar. "Nearly all jobs require training," he wrote. "Special instruction or practical experience—and sometimes both—is essential for achievement in almost all fields. Yet for the one occupation which sooner or later becomes the career of almost all women—that of housewife—there are no formal standards of proficiency whatever . . . nor are men much better prepared for their jobs as husbands."

More and more is being done to train people in marriage. For example, my minister coaches each young couple to expect the first year's clashes. He goes further—he tells them that by putting their creative heads together they can even outwit fate.

Chicago's Catholic churches offer a four-session course in marital preparation called "Pre-Cana Conference." These briefings cover practical problems such as money, food, and physical matters; but they major on the psychological aspects of marriage.

French Quebec is served by over 100 high schools called "Écoles Ménagères" which prepare girls for vocations, and especially for wifehood. The French natives refer to these institutions as "the schools of happy marriage."

In the United States, Stephens College leads all others in marital education. Less than one in 20 of its graduates has been divorced, as against the national record of one in three.

Dr. Lloyd W. Rowland, director of Louisiana's Society of Mental Health, is trying to teach "teeners" to learn about love before they leap. The backbone of his campaign is a series of superb pamphlets distributed to high-school girls and boys throughout that State.

Marriage counseling clinics are on the march, with Richmond, Virginia, in the van. Through that community's clinic, betrothed people are trained to tackle their marital job, and married people are shown how to unsnarl themselves. From two to six interviews are usually enough to put such couples back on the road to happiness. This service is largely supported by the Richmond Community Chest.

All such training might well pay more attention to the part that imagination can play in making our marriages prosper. Outsiders can help with their counsel, but there can be no surer way to solve our day-to-day problems than for us husbands and wives to use our creative minds. Only thus can we foresee friction, generate ideas to prevent strife, think up ways to restore amity, and set a positive course towards consistent serenity.

3.

The minding of our marital tongues is a creative problem, and a serious one. The Reverend John A. O'Brien of Notre Dame has frequently stressed the fact that many marriages are wrecked on verbal rocks. As counselor to couples he has often saved them from divorce by having them kneel and promise that, from then on, they will think twice before they speak once.

The problem is one of listening as well as talking. I asked a waiter at a New York hotel whether he wore his hearing aid at home. "Yes," he said, "so I can make my wife think I'm listening when it's shut off."

A young husband sank into his favorite chair after his evening meal to read his newspaper. Having washed the dishes, his wife of six months sat down opposite him, pulled out her knitting, and remarked:

"I went to see the doctor today."

He kept on reading. At long last, he abruptly looked up and genially replied:

"Oh, you *did*? How is *he*?"

Timing is of vital importance. A daily crisis in married life is the husband's homecoming. Bogged down by a day of boring housework it is natural for a wife to start complaining the minute her knight crosses the threshold. If she would but exercise her imagination, she would favor herself by saving her lamentations until later.

A wife met her husband at the airport with the family car. Before he had a chance to ask about his dog, she blurted: "Brutus was out all last night. Early this morning he awakened me with the worst howling I ever heard. You've got to get rid of him."

The man defended the old dog on the ground that he probably had found some girl friends. That made matters worse. All evening she kept blaming him for his dog's nocturnal sprees. Finally she arose from her favorite armchair and said, "I'm going to bed; aren't you?"

"No," he replied, "I'm going out with Brutus. We'll be back in the morning."

Husbands, however, are even more culpable at homecoming. Seldom do they ask, "What have you been doing today?" or more specifically: "How did that cake come out that you were going to bake?" If the husband has had a good day he is apt to boast. If he has had a bad day, he's too apt to sulk.

How easily such irritations could be avoided if we only gave a little advance thought as to what to talk about! To think up congenial topics might take a little effort, but might do much to foster marital harmony.

4.

Jacques Bacal reports that the big fact he learned from his years of counseling is that most marital shipwrecks are caused by "barnacles"—"by the accumulation of day-by-day irritations." One wife who made a success of her marriage told this story:

"As I look back over a glowingly successful marriage, I find that our happiness is mostly a matter of small personal adjustments. One of the first things I noted was that my husband left the cap off the toothpaste. That was a small enough thing, but it irritated me and I explained it to him. He now screws the cap on so tight that I have a hard time getting it off. This little adjustment is a symbol of other big adjustments which have made our life together a gallant and humorous one."

But a warning word is seldom sufficient. One happily married wife fretted over her husband's habit of putting his ashes into the saucer of his coffee cup. She had often chided him for this, but to no avail. Finally, she attacked the problem creatively and thought up a solution. At each meal she placed not one, but *three,* ashtrays in front of her husband. This pleasantly put an end to that vexation.

Similarly, William Feather reported: "I have done all I could to reduce domestic bickering. One contribution early in my married life was the purchase and delivery of two copies of our morning newspaper. Under this plan the stay-at-home had her paper, and the go-away-to-business had his."

And my partner, Bruce Barton, early adopted the plan of having his first-of-the-month salary check sent to his wife, and his middle-of-the-month check sent to him. Thus he eliminated any possible controversy about money. His feeling is that "a good marriage can stand wide differences of opinion on BIG things far better than the perpetual repetition of *petty* annoyances."

Getting along with relatives can likewise tax imagination. A New England woman took her mother-in-law into her home. The old lady's continued questioning got on her nerves. But she kept the peace while she thought up an antidote. "From now on," she announced to her in-law, "whenever you ask me about our private affairs, I will either lie to you or give you a nonsensical answer. Which would you prefer?" Luckily, the old lady had a sense of humor, so nonsense won. The strategy worked. The daughter-in-law recently reported, "The sillier my answer is, the more fun we get out of it—*both* of us."

Frontal attacks are seldom good tactics. When a husband bellows at his plump wife, "if you don't stop stuffing yourself you're going to look like an oversized sow," that kind of browbeating usually results in nothing but resentment. By contrast, Dr. Gayelord Hauser tells this story about how imagination can work wonders:

"A good husband helped his wife reduce by buying her a beautiful and expensive dress in the size she wore when he first fell in love with her. The dress hung in her wardrobe, waiting, a goal to be attained. The result was magical."

Whereas nagging tends to turn molehills into mountains, imagination can often do away with marital irritations. By brainstorming our "barnacles" with questions such as "How else?" "What else?" "When else?", we can enliven our creative minds and lengthen our honeymoons.

5.

A mother I know threw out these challenges to a group of young women: "Could you take that cold plunge to close the bedroom window? Could you make sure the clean towels are ready on his rack? Could you get his breakfast on the table in time and with the coffee steaming? Could you put a pie-crust on yesterday's meat and potatoes instead of serving fatigued leftovers? Could you think up the right questions to unlock the story of his business day?"

Then, too, just think of the many positive ways in which we men could brainstorm our husbandly duties. There's no end to the domestic benevolences we could think up and perform—if we only tried hard enough!

Any of us husbands could easily contrive countless acts of endearment along conventional lines; but we need to stretch our imaginations to think up extra touches, such as that illustrated by the story told by David Dunn about the elderly gentleman who goes out to his garden every summer morning, picks a single bloom of whatever is in flower, and takes it to his invalid wife. "The smile on her face as he presents it to her, and her exclamation of pleasure, are so genuine that an outsider would assume this was the first such attention she had ever received; yet the little ceremony is thirty summers old."

6.

Those are some of the little ideas which can cement marital relations. As for big ideas, all marriage counselors agree that little children do most to keep couples in harmony. Franklin P. Jones put an ironic twist on that fact: "Children often hold a marriage together—by keeping their parents too busy to quarrel with each other."

Metropolitan Life probably makes more studies of family relations than all other probers put together. Louis I. Dublin, Metropolitan's vice-president in charge of statistics, concludes: "Children cement family ties, and the earlier they come the better."

More and more psychologists believe that church-going is another big idea for making marriages last. While on the faculty of M.I.T., Alexander Magoun wrote a book entitled *Love and Marriage*. After 355 pages of scientific discussion, he concluded: "Every material problem is a spiritual problem. We should seek a better religion for better human relations within the family, exactly as we seek better physical things for better physical comfort in the home."

A man whom we will call John, after seven years of incompatability, broke with his wife whom we'll call Barbara. He happened upon the minister who had married them. They had never been to church since the wedding day. After several sessions with this minister, John persuaded Barbara to come back to him. And he thought up a way to ceremonialize their reunion. He arranged with that minister to marry them again, just as though they had never been wed.

Dr. John A. O'Brien tells about the father who thought

up a way to dramatize the need of changing shoes. Among their wedding presents, his son and his bride came across a pair of old brogues and a pair of evening slippers. They recognized them as their own old worn-out shoes. With these was an envelope containing a check and the following letter addressed to the groom:

"With this money please buy new shoes in which you and your wife can tread the path of married life. In the beginning, marriage, like these new shoes, can be a tight fit and may pinch. But as the days, weeks and years pass, you will find that your marriage grows more satisfying, more perfect—and as comfortable as the worn old shoes. I wish you both a pleasant journey. Your loving father."

Thus can imagination make its point without the taint of preachment.

7.

Marriage counselors might well emulate the imagination of Judge Thomas Cunningham, who presides at the Domestic Relations Court in Los Angeles. In almost every case that comes before him he seeks an idea for reconciliation and usually finds one. Here's his testimony:

"I stayed up nights trying to figure out some way to halt this growing tide of breakups. I was amazed at the trivial things that started arguments which ended in divorce. For instance, one man's chief complaint against his wife had been that she didn't make soup often enough, and a young woman sued for divorce because her husband made a 'clicking noise' with his false teeth."

Part IV of the Supreme Court of Erie County, N. Y., is known as the "Heartbreak Court," where over 2500 local couples have tried to sever their ties. The judge works like a master mechanic. He seeks ways to repair the trouble spots, and save the marriage. To dramatize the gravity of breakups he has hung a lone picture on the forward wall of his courtroom. It portrays a small, barefoot boy, poorly dressed, kneeling beside his bed and praying:

"Dear Lord, please make Mama and Papa stop fightin' because it's hard to take sides when you love them both, an' besides, I'm ashamed to face the other kids."

Any man or woman in marital trouble can think up ways to offset unhappiness and thus give marriage more time to mend itself. For instance, a husband became infatuated with a younger woman, and his wife was about to start divorce proceedings, when a friend of hers suggested that she take on new interests which might sublimate her distress. She listed 23 activities, out of which she chose the writing of poetry. This gave her a creative outlet which kept her going until her husband regained his senses.

Another woman on the verge of divorce made a parallel analysis of the pros and cons. This decided her against going to Reno. Instead, she worked up a list of alternatives, out of which she built a program of what she called "continued treatment"—a program of things for her to do both at home and outside. Through these creative efforts she vastly improved her marital relations.

Timing is a key to continuing marriage. And lapse of time heals many a rift, as Nina Wilcox Putnam pointed out in her personal story:

"Many times during the past twenty-three years my husband and I have faced down almost every conceivable ground for divorce. . . . Always one or both of us have taken time out for reflection, with the result that a better, stronger relationship has sprung from the ashes of our anger. I believe that in any marriage *time* is 'of the essence.'"

The use of time as a tool is but one of many ideas for solving marital problems. Imagination is not only "of the essence" but can be the *key* to successful marriage.

Chapter 20

CHILD TRAINING calls for

creative thinking

JOSHUA LOTH LIEBMAN, author of *Peace of Mind,*
wrote this warning when he was nearing his end:

"We must have in the home a system of 'checks and
balances' which will avoid, on the one hand, the extreme of
tyranny whereby the father plays the role of dictator, or
the mother stars as the omnipotent leading lady. At the other
extreme, our family democracy should avoid the anarchy in
which there are no laws, rules, responsibilities or disciplines.
Sons and daughters cannot develop their full potentialities
either in tyranny or anarchy."

Tyranny can be unimaginative; but a democracy which
combines discipline with freedom cannot exist without benefit of creative thinking at every turn.

We need to change shoes with our children, and to see
ourselves as they see us. We should do our best to foresee
trouble and nip it in the bud. We must think up solutions
of unpreventable problems. We even have to anticipate filial
strategies, and practice what J. P. McEvoy has called "the
art of out-foxing our children."

That all calls for active use of imagination. As Dr. W. W.
Bauer said in his book *Stop Annoying Your Children:* "Being
a good parent means *working* at it." And what better way to
work at it than to work our imaginations?

2.

According to Dr. William C. Menninger, "the best thing parents can do is to teach their children how to love." We should certainly do our utmost to achieve congeniality in the family circle, and to fight off friction. And yet a father I knew estranged his little son by taunting him continually. For instance, night after night at the dinner table the big man would ask the little boy, "Are you still the dumbest in your class?" If that father could only have foreseen the tragic result of his humorless razzing—if only he had used enough imagination to put himself into his little boy's shoes!

By contrast, a Chicago newspaperman, George B. Anderson, used his creative head and devised for his family a "fun" plan—a long-range program through which he and his wife and children have achieved a rollicking comradery. "I don't know of any family where parents and children are as close to each other as *they* are," a friend of theirs told me.

A big word in the lexicon of youth is *play*. If we can think up ways to make games of filial duties we can substitute congeniality for conflict. Forcing a child to take a noon-day rest is a frequent cause of friction. One mother I know solved this by thinking up a game to play with her little Susie. The mother lies down with her child and together they run movies through their heads, but with their eyes closed. When Susie's mother told me about that I asked her what their latest scenario was like. Here it is:

"We are at the beach. We are playing on the sand. Look at those gulls out there. What a noise they are making. Oh my! One of them just dove down and grabbed a poor little fish. Look, Mommy, see that freighter out there—so far away. It's got a long black tail—only the tail is pointing up toward the sky, and instead of having just one curl it has lots of curls. Oh look! Part of the tail just came off, and it's floating over toward that white cloud." . . . At about this point, Susie happily departed for dreamland.

Thinking up games to enliven chores can work well even with older children. At dinner's end, each night, a wise old friend of mine pulls out a deck of cards and deals poker hands to his three grown-up children. The winner is excused for that evening, while the other two jovially clear the table and do the dishes.

Another father has pitted his two big boys against each other in a friendly contest: One is "captain" of the cellar; the other is "captain" of the garage. Their dad inspects both domains every Saturday, and presents a token of victory to that week's winner.

Another challenge to imagination is to think up simple amusements. A young father faced the problem of keeping his son from loafing at the drugstore around the corner. He solved this very simply by installing a basketball net on his garage.

What to do to add fun to meals is well worth thinking up—even if it's only nonsense. A banker friend of mine purposely makes himself the butt of his children's laughter. Recently his wife told him during dinner: "Your spectacles are dirty." Silently, he took them off, sprinkled salt and pepper on the lenses, rubbed them with his napkin, placed his specs back upon his nose and pompously resumed eating.

The more we can brighten the home spirit, the better our family relations will be. And by trying to think up ways to that end, we parents can help develop our creativeness.

3.

An imaginative twist can make simple parties more exciting than if elaborate and expensive. The right kind of high jinks can even help solve child problems, as was demonstrated in a neighborhood which had become infested with gun-toting "cowboys" and "cowgirls" aged from three to seven.

Four of those swashbucklers were children of Mrs. William Vaughan, wife of a former ace in the F.B.I. She decided something should be done about the neighborhood "crime wave." "We ought to show our kids that *real* cowboys do more than just shoot," said Mrs. Vaughan to my daughter. "Let's see what we can think up."

On the next Saturday morning, their children marched up and down carrying placards announcing a backyard rodeo for that afternoon. The invitation stipulated, "Wear cowboy gear but bring no guns." The rodeo consisted of 12 events of which these four were typical:

Lasso the Steer: The props for this were a clothes-tree, and a lasso made from Mrs. Vaughan's clothes-line. One kid did succeed in throwing the noose over the hook, but all the others failed.

Bronco Busting: Here the horses were tricycles, and the "wild mustang" was a placid-faced clown of inflated rubber, about four feet tall. The children took turns—each riding at breakneck speed on his three-wheeled steed, then leaping onto the bronco and "rasseling" him to the earth.

Target Practice: The "guns" were little catapults, and the bullets were Ping-pong balls. A few kids hit the bull's-eye in the target painted on Mr. Vaughan's discarded shirt. But, on the whole, they found their aim far less deadly than when racing around the streets killing hombres right and left.

Grand Leap: The props for this were a ladder and a crib mattress. The older children were allowed to climb as high as they dared, as long as they jumped down from there. Strangely enough, the bully of the gang lost his nerve at the third rung.

That party gave the kids an exciting afternoon; and it gave them pause—made them wonder whether their shooting arms made them such big shots after all. And the planning of the occasion gave Mrs. Vaughan's creative mind a good workout. The entire afternoon for the 16 children cost only two quarts of apple juice, two boxes of crackers, and a few ounces of imagination.

The problem of how to keep children out of mischief on Halloween was solved by residents of Clarendon Place who put their heads together and worked up a street party. A parade of over 60 costumed children started at six in the evening. A committee awarded prizes for the best get-ups. After that came a picnic supper with hot dogs, hamburgers and ice cream. The older children were then organized into groups for square-dancing, while the younger ones were entertained by movies. This simple plan proved so successful that it is now an annual affair.

Since treasure hunts have fallen into conventional patterns, why not think up new twists? A neighbor did this for her daughter's birthday party at the beach. She planted surprise packages in the sand and marked each spot with a different flower. Then she gave each of her little guests a duplicate bud. I never saw such hilarity as when those 20 tots were running up and down the beach, each trying to find a blossom which would match the one he or she held in hand.

Or, how about a switcheroo? How about not only reversing the roles but even reversing the sexes? One mother did this when she thought up a "Scrambled Party." She had the girls come dressed as boys, and the boys dressed as girls. The merriment consisted of the males doing the things that females usually do, and vice versa. For one stunt she gave the girls cosmetics and had them make up the boys. Another event was a needle-threading contest for the young men.

So we're going to have a party for our children? Let's think up ways to make it different. Or better yet, let's team up with our young and jointly generate ideas. Such a session is sure to be fun and is likely to lead to new thoughts which can make that next party less elaborate, less expensive, and yet more memorable.

4.

Even discipline calls for imagination. There are ways to scold and ways not to scold. Before reprimanding we might well consider alternatives such as "Where else?" and "When else?" Curtain lectures make more of a dent when well-timed. It usually pays to wait until emotions have ebbed. And it is well to set the scene. For instance, parents can often get further with their children while walking with them than when towering over them at home.

How to dramatize a child's shortcoming is ever a creative challenge. A Mrs. C. G. Habley of Sherman Oaks, California, told me how one father uses his imagination along that line. Whenever his son fails to polish his own shoes, the father shines just one shoe of each of the boy's pairs. Surely that's a far better idea than nagging!

A lawyer friend of mine had boys of 10 and 12 who quarreled all through the Christmas holidays. For New Year's he bought each of them a surprise present. But before receiving this, each son had to sign an agreement which their father had drawn up. This stipulated the different ways in which the boy had irritated his brother, and ended with a promise that he would turn over a new leaf for the new year. The dad made a ceremony of the signing of these formidable documents, with the mother inking in her signature as witness.

In parental problems the idea we seek may sometimes be found in the realm of turning the tables. A young couple conceived a plan along this line to break their little ones of the habit of invading the living room after they had been put to bed upstairs. The next night when the two tots appeared in their nighties they were ignored. The mother turned to her husband and said, "Well, I think it's time to go to bed." The parents arose, turned off the lights and went upstairs. You can imagine how well that little idea worked.

When we imaginatively discipline our children we help insure the desired result with less danger to amity than when we bawl them out. And by trying to think up these strategies we parents not only tend to keep our homes happier but also to keep our imaginations wider awake.

5.

If we cannot spare the rod, we can at least think up better ways to spank. As in scolding, it is better if we pick the right time and place instead of letting our ire tell us when and where.

Even a bit of drama may pay off. One of Canada's legal lights has three little boys; and ever since they could be expected to know right from wrong their father has taken care of the spanking duties. But for each such session he always puts on a garment which he wears at no other time— a wild and woolly sport coat. When a boy needs punishment he says, "Well, I guess I'll have to go upstairs and put on my spanking jacket." That helps make his whacks more telling.

We also need imagination to make the punishment fit the crime—to deal out penalties which the child will deem fair. The Dale Castos do this by changing places. They sit down with their son and carefully discuss the issue. Then they put it up to him to decide what the punishment should be. At one session, the penalty he chose was such that his father found himself saying: "Son, we think you're being too hard on yourself. Instead of not playing ball for a whole week, we think a two-day layoff will be penalty enough."

In contrast, Dr. W. W. Bauer told about a little boy who was late for lunch. "The mother flew at him in a fury, berated him as a little beast and then forced him to eat his food—all of it." After she went out, the boy vomited. That night the parents could not find him. At midnight the police called to report that they had caught the tot trying to hitch-hike out of town.

Here's what his mother should have done, according to Dr. Bauer: "When lunchtime came and Joe did not appear, she should have eaten her lunch and cleared it away. Then when Joe arrived she should have told him to get his own lunch and to clear up afterward. This would have fitted his offense and would have taught him that it didn't pay to be late for meals."

6.

We parents can bring up our own creative power by trying to bring out the creative best in our offspring. For one thing, we can set an example. When I discussed this with Mrs. William Gerber she told me:

"Thank goodness I was fortunate enough to have parents with wide-awake imaginations. One incident comes to mind: When I was about 12, my hair was like a mop. One morning I could find neither barrette nor bobby pin to keep it out of my eyes. I flew into a tantrum. Finally my father suggested I use large safety pins. In desperation I did, and they worked. I learned then not only to use my imagination but to dare to be different."

When our children are too young to do things for themselves, it is well to have them watch our creative efforts. Peter Hunt recommends that, in the presence of our little ones, we make gay things for their playroom. Thus we can fan their creative spark and incidentally give them a good time.

And it can be fun for Daddy, too. When my first daughter was a little girl, I decided to build her a doll-house. We spent evening after evening together in our cellar while I improvised and carpentered. I shudder now to think how ambitious a project that was! Who ever heard of a doll-house completely covered with shingles no bigger than thumb-nails?

Better still, let's have our children join with us in creative effort as soon as they are old enough. A dear friend of mine encourages his little son's imagination by swapping stories with him—original tales that have to be made up on the spot. He told me: "When I used to make up yarns for my kids, all they did was listen. Then I hit on the idea of bargaining. Now I say to my child, 'It isn't fair for me to make up all the stories, so here's what we'll do—I'll tell you two stories for every one you tell to me.'"

Most youngsters like to take things apart but seldom try to put them back together. I know a father who lets his son pull machines to pieces and then teams up with him in re-assembling them. Another friend of mine built a four-bedroom summer cottage with no helpers other than his sons, aged 10 and 12. In their workshop that dad and his boys produce almost everything from sailboats to derricks.

Sometimes, however, we might better induce our children to tackle something creative on their own than to collaborate with them too much. For when we try to do our children's thinking for them we tend to pauperize their minds. Whenever a child of Mrs. Jean Rindlaub gets restless and whines, "What is there for me to do?" Mrs. Rindlaub's answer is always something like this:

"Come on, Anne—get a pad of paper, take a pencil and write down all the things you might like to do. I'll bet you could think up at least 25. And you'll find that just by writing down that list you'll have lots of fun."

Department store executive Julian Trivers likewise believes in making his youngsters think up. One evening at dinner he unwrapped a mysterious wooden box with a slot in it. He then told his five children about suggestion systems such as are used in about 6000 businesses, and he announced that each child was to think up ideas for the family good and stick them in that box. He then described the entrancing prizes which would be awarded at the end of each month for the best suggestions. The Trivers system didn't create any earth-rocking ideas; but it did help teach the five Triverettes that they were blessed with minds which were meant for creative *use*.

7.

Those are some of the everyday ways in which we parents might well use more imagination. But an older child may sometimes bring home a problem so calamitous that we must either solve it in time, or risk ruining the life of our son or daughter, not to mention our own lives. In such crises our creativity may be our main hope.

When a son commits a crime such as driving without a license and maiming somebody, I know of no greater challenge to a father's creative power than to see his son through that kind of Hell—and to salvage him.

When a child makes a tragic mistake in mating, the parents are faced with a task that taxes their minds beyond anything else in their lives. In one such case where a California girl eloped with a rotter, her father spent the best part of three months trying to think up how to undo her error. Success finally came through his brainstorming the "who-elses?" He hit upon the idea of hiring a lawyer who had been trained in the F.B.I., and who knew how to dig up the records which finally proved the male gold-digger to be a bigamist.

In such crises we can either let our emotions strangle our mentalities, or we can recognize our problems to be the *creative* challenges that they *are*, and attack them as such. Thus we can at least *try* to think through to happier endings.

Chapter 21

HOME CHORES less humdrum

when creatively attacked

ALFRED TOOMBS took over his wife's housekeeping duties in order to prove to her how easy it was to run their home. After the first day he realized why Mother Nature had saved women from beards—"no housewife could possibly find time to shave." At the end of a week he concluded: "Housekeeping is the toughest job I've ever tackled. It requires use of all the known muscles."

Including the *imaginative* muscles! For if a woman goes at it right, she can use her home as a gym wherein to exercise her creativity—and be a better housekeeper to boot.

The fact is that the domestic duties of most wives call for more imaginative effort than do the cut-and-dried jobs of their husbands. "What can I make out of these left-overs?" . . . "How can I get Johnny to bed on time?" . . . "Whom can we find to sit for us this Saturday evening?" On such questions many a woman can, and does, whet her creative wits—day in and day out, from sunrise to lights-out.

In addition to that kind of mental activity, domestic chores should encourage the incubation of ideas. When alone in a quiet home—manually going through motions which have become second nature—a woman can meditate as well as she could in an ivory tower. By directing her musing toward a specific goal, rather than letting it run hog-wild, a homekeeper can think up solutions to family problems, and incidentally help keep her imagination in trim by so doing.

2.

Shopping certainly calls for agile thinking; and the leaner the purse the more imagination it takes. A husband may look upon meat-buying, for example, as a simple routine; but when he sits down to a goulash as tasty as tenderloin but costing far less, he should thank his lucky stars that his wife has used her imagination instead of his dollars.

Any woman who creatively attacks the almost daily task of food buying is helping to keep her mind imaginative. She must look ahead and think up alternatives beyond the obvious, every time she plans a meal. One of the ablest housewives I know spoke thus to a group of women:

"Are your meals attractive in color? In taste? Are they nutritious and balanced? Why not try something new instead of serving the same old things day after day? Shop at your food store as if every meal were to be a party. Use your creative imagination in your meal-planning and you'll find yourself blessed."

A woman doctor, otherwise unable to induce her five-year-old daughter to eat enough food, finally asked the child personally to plan the family's suppers for a whole week. This strategy worked like magic. Surprisingly enough the child's menus called for fewer of the costly meats than she had usually demanded.

By stretching her imagination a woman can stretch her dollars when shopping for clothes. And it is well if she foresees how she will look to others in what she buys. A Southern girl, Bonnie Driscoll, came to New York to produce fashion shows. She soon realized that Eastern women looked different. So, when selecting a dress, she asked herself, "How would I feel if I were wearing this costume and should happen to bump into the Duchess of Windsor?"

"The chances of my meeting the Duchess of Windsor were about one in a million," she told me, "but the mental hoop I put my mind through by imagining that crisis saved me from taking on many a '*dog*.' And, believe it or not, I later *did* bump into the Duchess of Windsor!"

3.

Cooking! Who ever heard of a good cook not using plenty of ingenuity?

Sometimes, however, a wife may *mis*use her imagination in regard to her cooking duties by thinking of herself as an ugly drudge sweating over a hot stove. She should see herself as her mates sees her; for every right-minded husband would agree with Thomas Wolfe: "There is no spectacle on earth more appealing than that of a beautiful woman in the act of cooking dinner for someone she loves."

Many famous writers, actors, and painters practice the culinary art. They recognize cooking as a truly creative exercise. Almost every dish calls for thinking up some way to make it tempting. And there is no limit to the recipes we can invent.

A highly trained member of the Betty Crocker staff pointed out to me that when her associates were putting together the new *Betty Crocker Cookbook*, they were amazed to find how many of the best recipes had been contributed by amateurs. That's why the book is so filled with credits to people who are truly creative but who probably don't know that they are.

Cooking calls for the usual idea-begetting questions, such as "What else?" and "How else?", and also for other questions such as "What other shape?" Mrs. Maynard F. Soule, of New Hampshire, is one of many who have thought up new forms for old foods. When her son Danny was about to celebrate his seventh birthday, she made him a cake in the shape of a train. She pushed back the top layer of one section so that it would slant like a locomotive, frosted its top and sides, and then mounted on top of that a smokestack made of "Lifesavers." The headlight was a bright red candy. The boxcar was frosted yellow and the caboose red. For the wheels on the engine and on the cars, she used round chocolate cookies.

In culinary creativity the choice of ingredients is boundless. For example, Mrs. Clayton Andrews, of Clinton, Nebraska, has created a Rose Petal Jam. Her recipe starts like this: "Gather fresh rose blossoms in early morning. Cut away the base and heel of each flower; wash and drain well. To each cup of petals add one cup of water and one cup of sugar. Boil until sugar hardens on a wooden spoon. Add a few drops of lemon juice," etc.

And listen to Margaret Broadley: "The best mince pie I ever ate was made by a conservative New England woman, all of whose recipes came out of her head. She gave the final fillip to that famous mince pie of hers with a handful of coffee grounds."

In thinking up what to cook and how to cook it—in thinking up new ingredients and new shapes—in every aspect, cooking can challenge imagination; and when tackled creatively it can serve to enliven our minds.

4.

We can help keep ourselves keen by thinking up better ways to keep things clean. Even dusting can do with a bit of imagination.

Dishwashing? There's always another and a better way; and there's a creative plus to this chore which we men should recognize. We know that our ideas pop best while we are shaving. The same absence of distraction, soothing sound of running water (and, yes, the heat) likewise tend to help us cook up ideas while doing dishes. Personally, I have helped at the kitchen sink several evenings a week throughout my married life. I know from experience that many an idea for which I had been groping during the day has come to me while scraping a plate or polishing a goblet.

Whitney Williams reports that one of Hollywood's top scripters, stumped for ideas, takes out the family vacuum cleaner and cleans rugs all over the house. This chore relaxes his imaginative muscles—flexes his mind so that he can go back to his creative chores with renewed power.

Laundry work? Even this offers women an opportunity to exercise imagination. An authoress told me: "I can do my best creative thinking while ironing. Any activity which keeps the eyes occupied in one spot, while leaving the mind relatively free, is a distinct aid to mental concentration. In a way it is like fixing the eyes on a single light, as is done in hypnosis."

And laundering is beset with little problems which challenge imagination. For instance, a New Jersey woman loved loopy hooked rugs but detested the marks which clothespins left on them. So she thought up the new stunt of sewing a four-inch piece of muslin on each side before she put them in the tub.

Bed making seems like a cut-and-dried activity; but even this can be creatively attacked, as was proved by a Buffalo woman. She figured that the average housewife annually walks four miles and spends 25 hours just making one bed; so she thought up a way to cut the distance to a little over a mile and cut the time to 16 hours per year. Here's her one-trip bedmaking plan:

"Start at the head, smooth and tuck in one corner completely, from bottom sheet to bedspread. Move to the foot on the same side, tuck in that corner and work across the footboard. Now move up the opposite side, from bottom corner to top." This does away with detouring from head to foot and side to side—just one circuit and the bed is made.

Outwitting pests is often a poser to homekeepers. When bugs are immune to the usual poisons, what to do?

At a summer home in Canada, our hostess thought up an anti-insect campaign and put on a "Catch-the-Ant" contest while we were visiting there. In her kitchen she had hung up a colored scoreboard on which she had listed the seven members of her family, including Sleepy, the long-eared beagle. Pencilled check-marks recorded how many ants each contestant captured each day. Before we left, the mother had 68 ants to her credit; her son Teddy had 53; while Sleepy had just two. There was even some suspicion that Sleepy had had an assist from Teddy.

5.

We can also think creatively on how to make our homes safer and more livable. A neighbor recommends a "Comfort Tour" on which a housewife would ask herself: "What could I do to this room to make it cosier?" . . . "Are the ashtrays near the chairs?" . . . "Are pillows where they're needed?" . . . "Are there footstools for short people?" . . . "Are magazines and books in easy reach?" . . . "Are the lights of the right height and rightly placed?" Thus, room by room, a homekeeper could devise ways to enhance comfort.

A man and wife could think up at least one new idea a week to make their home more livable. Most of these improvements would be trivial, but they might hit upon something novel, as did Mrs. Anna Schisler. Her kitchen table, sink, and counters varied too much in height; so she bought an old piano stool and painted it white. By raising or lowering this she can now sit down to her work at just the right level.

In the home of a friend I noticed that the side of the Frigidaire served as a bulletin board. How? Simply by using magnetized disks to hold pieces of paper against the refrigerator's steel wall. The array included shopping lists, memos of appointments, and even clippings of cartoons that might amuse the family.

Sometimes an idea for greater convenience calls for an alteration, like the one thought up by a New York woman whose family harmony was marred by a towel problem. She had her husband construct a linen closet between the bathroom and the bedroom, with an opening into each room. The door to the bath is of glass and handy to the tub. By this simple idea she made sure that towels are always within reach, even when the bathroom is occupied.

Good ideas can be so simple that they sound almost silly. A Mrs. Mewhinney was tired of pulling the wrong rope to close or open her Venetian blinds; so she thought up the little stunt of tying a tiny piece of colored ribbon to the cord that closes the blinds. Even her little children know that when they want to open them, they pull the ribbonless cord.

Accident prevention is likewise a challenge to imagination. We might well make periodic "Safety Tours" to check up on wiring, on scatter rugs, on floor wax, on the strength of our stepladders, and on whatever might court accident or fire.

The main point is to anticipate. When we notice a pair of shoes on the stairway we should foresee a loved one tumbling down the steps head-first. When we see a carving knife left within easy reach of a child we should look ahead to what that might mean. When we see piles of newspapers in the cellar, we should fore-hear a fire engine sirening down the street toward our house.

6.

How about a Beauty Tour? On this round, we should ask ourselves: "What could I do to make this room more attractive?" . . . "What junk could I eliminate?" . . . "Should I rearrange the furniture?" . . . "Should I get that picture reframed?" . . . "Could I add a spot of color?"

Rearrangement calls for countless alternatives. We can avoid lugging heavy pieces from here to there and back again if we use our creative heads the way one woman did. She simply drew a map of each room on the scale of one foot to an inch. Then she cut out proportionate bits of colored paper to represent each piece of furniture. By moving these about with her fingers she could arrive at new lay-outs while sitting at her desk. The same idea could be used in furnishing a bare room.

An even better scheme was thought up by Paul Mac-Alister, who created a "Plan-a-Room" kit which contains 75 miniatures of furniture, cut to scale out of plain wood. By painting each of these little pieces, we can use them to visualize color schemes as well as arrangements.

When it comes to planting, the sky's the limit—as demonstrated by a woman living in a Park Avenue penthouse. She yearned for the country; so she created a diminutive farm right at her lofty doorstep. Instead of the usual flowers and shrubs, she planted tomatoes, corn, radishes, eggplant, berry bushes, and even little apple trees in yellow tubs. Some of her chairs are made out of cider barrels, and stools out of 10-gallon milk cans. The dining table is a huge wooden horseshoe which once adorned a blacksmith's shop in Maine. Tables made from hobbyhorses hold magazines and ashtrays and books. Wooden decoys serve as footstools.

Accessories for home beautification call for plenty of imagination. One woman, instead of covering her flowerpots, has merely polished them. Even window shades need not be drab, as was proved by a Philadelphia housewife who painted the inside of her shades in the colors which would add to the charm of each room.

We can use imagination in thinking up the size, character, color and framing of pictures. And in this phase of home beautification, ideas can take the place of dollars. Mrs. Edward Cart needed something to brighten up the plain green walls of her apartment and conceived the scheme of using a scenic fabric based on paintings by Grandma Moses.

Out of this cloth she cut single pictures, and framed each of them with neat black wood.

7.

Many a useful invention has been created by a home-maker who, in going about her housework, has run into a little problem which has spurred her into thinking up a worthwhile gadget. For instance, a Louisiana woman could not wash bottles as clean as she thought they should be; so she invented a special brush with a twist in the handle so that it could be expanded after insertion in a bottle, thus making it easier to clean both the bottom and the sides. Likewise, a Pennsylvania woman, incensed at the fumes which belched from her furnace each time it was stoked, devised a coal shovel with enough perforations to screen out the fine dust which caused the gaseous odors.

My friend Chandler Wells, a leading insurance specialist, was doing some painting at home and found that he couldn't keep his brush from messing the outside of the can; so he invented and patented a disk which fits the top of almost any container and prevents dripping.

Mrs. Dorothy Rodgers, wife of the famous Rodgers of Rodgers and Hammerstein, deplored the fact that although nearly every other home-cleaning chore had been improved, housewives still had to scour toilet bowls with brushes which, in turn, had to be cleaned, and even then were unsightly if not germy. So she thought up a toilet mop with a disposable head which could be released and flushed away after it had done its job.

The holder is a forceps-like handle of crystal-clear styrene plastic. Into the end of this the housewife slips a paper envelope containing a cellulose pad and impregnated with a detergent. She just swishes this around the bowl and then flicks it off by opening the handle. The pad goes down the drain, the toilet bowl sparkles, and the cost is less in the long run than former methods entailed. Called "Jonny Mop," this device is being made and marketed by the Personal Products Corporation.

Miss Lee Brower, private secretary to one of my associates, makes a hobby of dressmaking during her leisure hours at home. She likes frequent changes of costume and loves buttons. She put her mind to changing garb by changing buttons, and came up with an idea good enough to be patented—interchangeable buttons which, through color and shape, can transform an office dress into a dining-out gown in less time than it takes to powder a nose.

Even baby-sitting can lend itself to creative effort. This claim of mine was challenged by one of my married daughters. She and her husband wanted to attend a dance one Saturday. On Friday evening she seductively approached me: "Daddy, we can't find anybody to sit for us tomorrow night. Why don't you do it as an experiment to prove that baby-sitting can be as creatively productive as you say it can be?"

"Okay, I'll do it at the rate of $10 an hour—not to be paid by you, but by someone else," I recklessly boasted.

Luckily I had 24 hours in which to think up that evening's project—a piece for *Sales Management Magazine*. I wrote this during the three and a half hours in which I baby-sat, and sent it to the editor with a demand for $35. Ray Bill accepted it and wrote me as follows:

"You certainly get the gold crown as a high-priced baby-sitter. We are happy to remit the amount specified, with the understanding that you can use this $35 for any purpose you desire, including the hiring of a substitute baby-sitter the next time your daughter tries to rope you in."

That triumph puffed me up. But my pride was punctured when I read about 81-year-old Mrs. Fannie G. Smith, of Springfield, Massachusetts, who baby-sits about three nights a week. Does she twiddle her thumbs while doing so? No.

She invents new designs for mittens. She has scores of original patterns to her credit as a result of combining creativity with custodianship.

*   *   *

Homekeeping is less humdrum when looked upon as a series of creative challenges. The more imagination a woman puts into her domestic arts, the better she succeeds; and by striving to think creatively she can't help but keep herself mentally more alert, and therefore more attractive, as the years go on.

Chapter 22

JOBS are opportunities

for use of imagination

WE CAN NOT ONLY get ahead faster by applying imagination to our jobs but can help brighten our working hours. The more self-expression we put into our toil, the more self-realization we get out of it.

Being a railroad cop could be boring except during times of trouble; but T. M. Brown, lieutenant of police on the Erie Railroad, found a way to enliven his peaceable hours by starring as a magician.

Too many children were losing their lives on the Erie tracks. As an offset to this problem Lieutenant Brown thought up an educational entertainment designed to sell safety—a traveling show of magic, with him as the Houdini. School principals all along the line were glad to book his program for their assemblies; and no child could hear it and see it without thinking twice before trespassing again on Erie's right of way. Within one year, the death rate was cut in two.

The job of cutting children's hair could be a drudgery, but my friend Charlie has turned his barbershop into a barrel of fun for himself and for his juvenile patrons. Three generations of children have insisted that their parents take them there for their haircuts. Why? Because Charlie fascinates them with his home-made monkey tales. Stuffed monkeys adorn his shop, and he pretends that his basement is full of live monkeys (which nobody can ever see "because they're too bashful.")

2.

All professions call for creative imaginations. It is the very essence of science, according to Dr. James B. Conant.

In his economic classic, *The Wealth of Nations,* Adam Smith told this story: "In the first steam-engines, a boy was constantly employed to open and shut alternatively the communication between the boiler and the cylinder, according as the position either ascended or descended. One of those boys observed that by tying a string from the handle of the valve which opened this communication, to another part of the machine, the valve would open and shut without his assistance." Thus an historic improvement came from the imagination of an untrained mind. The annals of inventions abound with similar cases.

The practice of medicine is a continual challenge to imagination. In diagnosis, a doctor must conceive all possible alternatives. Although he can now lean upon instruments and testing procedures which the creative minds of others have devised, he cannot diagnose well unless he forces himself to think up plenty of hypotheses. And when it comes to treatment, here, again, he cannot go solely by book, but must apply his knowledge imaginatively.

Creativity helps explain the brilliancy of surgical progress. For example, instead of the sponge so often left in wounds after operations, we now have "vanishing sponges"—a new kind of cellulose which can be sewed up inside incisions and forgotten.

For further example, Dr. George N. Papanicolaou has thought up new "smear tests" to detect cancer. One of his problems was to obtain scrapings from the stomach. For this purpose he created a long thin tube of two channels leading to a soft balloon covered with delicate tassels. The patient swallows the balloon, which is then inflated inside the stomach and gently rubbed against the stomach wall. When deflated and taken out, the specimens absorbed by the little tassels are then tested.

On every call a physician needs to turn on his vicarious imagination—to put himself into his patient's shoes. The therapeutic value of this is dramatized in a story about the son of Lord Halifax. A veteran of World War II and a double amputee, he was asked to buck up a legless veteran who was too despondent to help rehabilitate himself. Some weeks later the head of the hospital told Halifax that the veteran was well on his way to recovery. "How did you do so much to restore his spirits?" the doctor asked. "That's easy to understand," said Halifax. "He saw that I was in his shoes!"

Doctors who serve children need especially to use imagination in their patient relations. As a newspaperman in my early days in Buffalo I heard a lot about a Doctor Borzilleri, who was the idol of that city's large and highly respected Italian colony. The other day I met his daughter, now the wife of a Marine colonel. I happened to tell her about Charlie the barber.

"Why," she said, "when my dad was a young practitioner, he had a non-existent animal, too. It was a dog with its tail in *front*. Whenever he had to treat a sick child, he would distract its attention by telling about this strange pet. Too often the child would insist on seeing the animal, and as a result my mother had to buy scores of toy dogs, cut off their tails, and sew them on their noses."

Dr. Lee L. Mulcahy, of Batavia, New York, has reduced children's dread of dentistry by means of a locomotive in his waiting room. It is a fascinating replica of the famed 1885 engine of the Atchison, Topeka & Santa Fe. Tiny tots sit on the tender with their feet in the cab, and ring the bell and work the gadgets. A little idea like that can do a lot to attract trade and lighten labor.

3.

How about pastors? Can you imagine the creative effort they must put into preparing a new sermon each week? Then, too, a successful minister has to use his ingenuity in raising money, in planning programs, in pleasing his flock and in countless other ways.

As to lawyers, a legal light remarked to me: "Give me a young graduate who has had only fair marks in school but has shown that he can think creatively, and I will make a better lawyer out of him than if he were an unimaginative valedictorian."

Lawyers certainly have to think up strategies, and to foresee what their adversaries will contend. And what a strenuous challenge to creativity a jury can be!

Professional artists? Imagination is the essence of their craft but they also can use imagination in their client relations. A prominent painter, after 40 years of portraiture, boasted to a young colleague: "I've never had a complaint from a subject!" When asked his secret he replied: "I always put myself in the model's shoes; I imagine how he would like to look and then I paint him that way!"

When recently I went to Jean Raeburn to be photographed, I could quickly see why he is going places as a portrayer of hard-to-take men. For example, instead of saying, "Smile," he suggests: "Now think of something pleasant." The result is a natural twinkle, instead of an artificial smirk.

Professional politicians have long followed conventional patterns in their campaigning; but Thomas Dewey had to think up something new to win the governorship of New York State in 1950. The odds were overwhelmingly against him; and yet overnight he reversed the tide by using a new medium in a brand-new way. All day long and all evening, he appeared before his vast television audience, extemporaneously answering questions that came in from voters all

over the state. Many of those who heard and saw him marveled at his grasp of public problems and decided to change
their ballots in his favor.

In the military profession, the strategies and tactics are
everything; and they depend upon creative thinking. A military leader must also put himself into his enemies' boots.
During the nip-and-tuck of the African campaign, General
Montgomery kept on the wall of his mobile headquarters a
photo of General Rommel. When asked why, Monty replied:
"So I can look at his picture and keep pondering, 'What
would I do if I were he?'"

In that same vein, Douglas Southall Freeman tells about
General Robert E. Lee's reaction to the replacement of Mc-
Clellan by Burnside as general of the enemy forces. The news
was received by Lee with mixed feelings. He was sorry that
his old associate of the Mexican War was no longer to oppose
him. "We always understood each other so well," he said to
Longstreet. "I fear they may continue to make these changes
till they find someone whom I don't understand."

4.

If a business is to survive in a competitive economy its
managers must likewise put themselves into the shoes of their
rivals. The relatively recent upsurge in market research has
been largely due to the desire of business heads to get a
better line on their competitors, to put themselves into the
shoes of their prospects, and to see themselves as the public
sees them. Such factual findings are usually useful to the
degree that they are imaginatively interpreted—translated
into ideas and into action.

Many a business has grown great through the kind of
creative thinking which Thomas Lipton exemplified. Starting
as a little butcher in Glasgow, Scotland, he made himself
stand out by wearing white overalls, immaculately starched.
He startled his thrifty neighborhood by illuminating his store

each night by gas. His signboard was a jumbo ham made out of wood and swiveled so that it would swing with the wind.

To cover a wider range, Lipton scrubbed up two fat porkers, decorated them with colored ribbons, and led them through Glasgow's streets with this legend painted on their sides: "We're going to Lipton's, the best shop in town for Irish bacon."

As he opened more shops he thought up more and bigger stunts. His masterpiece was the largest cheese in the world. This was paraded through the city during early December. Then, just before Christmas, he filled it with gold pieces. When it was finally cut up on Christmas Eve, the excitement ran as high as at the Irish Sweepstakes.

Food-selling may call for imagination, but how about banking? Until I became a bank director, I always felt that the success of a financial institution depended almost wholly on judicial judgment. But now I know that even in the granting of large loans, a banker who can think creatively will win out against an unimaginative competitor.

Then, too, unexpected exigencies in the banking business often call for quick-thinking ingenuity. My associate Alan Ward tells how his father once stopped a group of newly arrived Italians from making a run on his rural bank. One of these immigrants had seen the only local manufacturer withdrawing his weekly payroll in cash and had immediately started the rumor that the tycoons were "taking their money out of the bank." The Italian housewives rushed in to demand their families' funds. President Ward happened to know that they carried their money in the ample tops of their stockings, so he ordered his tellers to pay them in silver dollars. While the ladies milled around in bafflement over how to carry away so much heavy metal, Mr. Ward rounded up a leader of the Italian community who addressed the women in their native tongue and ended the stampede.

Rudyard Kipling's epic poem The "Mary Gloster" told

about an old shipbuilder named McCullough who had started at scratch and had become the leader in his line. On his deathbed he proclaimed that his success was due to the fact that, although his competitors could copy all of his innovations, "they couldn't copy my mind. And I left 'em sweating and stealing, a year and a half behind."

Kipling thus dramatized the fact that the importance of ideas in business cannot be exaggerated.

5.

Aptitude testers maintain that the two traits most needed for success in selling are an objective personality and creative imagination.

A salesman is like a football player in that he must be both a good carrier-out of plays as planned by the home office and a smart broken-field runner on his own. In his catch-as-catch-can grapples with prospects, he must think up one little idea after another. These are the *tactics* of selling. The strategy of selling is the planning—the *creative* planning which we do in advance of an interview.

After a long drive I reached my hotel in Rochester one night at about nine. I had previously made a date with myself to devote an hour before retirement to thinking up how to persuade my prospect the next day. During the evening I piled up and jotted down ideas. My next morning's interview succeeded, largely because of the creative thinking I had done the night before. That victory happened to be a turning-point in my business career.

A vice-president in charge of purchases told me about a salesman who had long called on him without landing a single order. "He never got discouraged. Each time I turned him down, he'd just smile and say he'd try it again. Eventually I found myself giving him over $100,000 worth of business a year. What won me over? It was his habit of giving me an idea each time he called."

If a man on the road keeps his imagination awake he can capture ideas that can help his home office. For example, G. Cullen Thomas, General Mills Vice-president and Director of Product Control, reported this case:

"One of our salesmen sent us some partially-baked dinner rolls that he had picked up at a small bakeshop in Florida. They were blond, almost white in color, anything but appetizing. But when we reheated them to complete their bake, we had delicious, hot rolls with a delightful home-made flavor. We immediately secured the rights to this simple process and turned it over to our research and technical personnel for further experimental study. About eight weeks later, we were able to present to the baking industry the revolutionary 'Brown 'n' Serve' bakery products that have since won their way into millions of American homes."

Thus an imaginatively alert salesman can be a long arm of his company's creative research.

6.

In days of old many an employee was pushed ahead by relatives who owned the business or by bankers who loaned to it; but that royal road is a rarity nowadays. In nearly every case the man who now rises toward the top is propelled by two forces: (1) His superiors want to pull him up to work with them because they need his help. (2) His immediate associates want to shove him up because they believe in him *and like him*. If he lacks creative energy his superiors won't covet him. If he lacks vicarious imagination his associates won't cotton to him.

It's a rare employee who can envision his firm's need for economy. A company president who is personally open-handed recently complained to me: "During the course of the year I have hundreds of requests from our people for this or that expenditure, but hardly anyone ever comes to me with a suggestion as to how we could save money." Just think how favorably one of his young men could make himself stand out by thinking up some money-saving ideas!

It strains imagination but little to think up ways to find things out; and yet the failure to do just that has held back many an employee. A Sears, Roebuck executive recently remarked to me: "We take on the brightest minds we can find, but too often our new employees are helpless when called upon for something beyond their routine. They seem to have no inkling as to how to go about looking up this or that." Thus many a boss hungers for more ingenuity on the part of his people.

Carl E. Holmes, business consultant, believes that most employees stand still because of their creative shortcomings. "God gave us imagination," says Mr. Holmes, "and imagination can be the most potent force in our lives, yet few use it constructively. . . . Knowledge is a good thing, industry is a good thing, but imagination is a miracle worker."

7.

Some 6000 American companies operate suggestions systems through which their 20,000,000 employees are urged to submit ideas for the good of the business and are well rewarded for acceptable suggestions. This movement is our nation's only major effort designed to keep our people on their creative toes.

Said Henry Ford II: "We Americans are becoming more and more a nation of employees. Four out of five people today work for somebody else. The job of distributing management is one of the special problems of our times." That fact alone justifies the millions which employers are annually investing in suggestions systems.

And there's another reason, according to Harry J. Richey of the National Biscuit Company: "A suggestions system offers the last means of direct communication between top management and the man on the production line—a way to recognize and develop leadership. National Biscuit makes the bulk of its promotions from those who offer suggestions."

An executive of the Eastman Kodak Company points out still another virtue of suggestions systems: "In these programs both the employee and the company have much to gain and nothing to lose. The fundamental basis is therefore friendly. Improved labor relations obviously result, to the benefit of *both*."

Suggestions systems are growing ever greater. In just one year the amount paid to Eastman Kodak employees for their ideas increased by $28,000 to a new high of $191,000. A total of 9711 suggestions were adopted, a gain of 1100 over the previous year. In one Kodak plant, last year, four individuals submitted more than 50 ideas each.

In 1951 the General Electric Company paid to employees for their ideas an average of over $50,000 a month.

The size of award depends upon the value of the suggestion. Cash prizes range upward from five dollars to small fortunes. Many companies have paid $5000 or more for one idea. A suggestion champion by name of Charles Zamiska, received over $28,000 for devising a better way to handle cores in the casting department of the Cleveland Graphite Bronze Company. That sum represented 25 per cent of the resultant savings during the first six months.

The average cost of installing and operating suggestions systems runs about $6 per year per employee. Processing costs range from $4 to $25 per suggestion. It has been estimated that American businesses are investing over $100,-000,000 a year in these programs. Surveys show that 27.6 per cent of the ideas suggested are worth accepting and awarding.

But—it takes ideas to get ideas; and unless enough creative imagination is put into running a suggestions system it is likely to fail. For example, in a Bendix division some 2500 employees were so apathetic that they submitted a total of only four suggestions a week. The system was brought back to life by showmanship. Instead of drab suggestions boxes,

"Idea Banks" with "tellers' windows" were installed all over the plant. Blinking signs beckoned the workers. The suggestion blanks became "deposit slips," and the acknowledge forms became "bank statements." The committee in charge of awards became the "Board of Directors of the Idea Bank." Within two months the inflow of suggestions from those Bendix employees increased 30-fold.

* * *

The success of suggestions systems proves that almost any of us can think up more ideas on our jobs. And it is well-nigh axiomatic that—whether we be employees, employers or professional people—the more imagination we put into our work, the more we prosper. And isn't it just as obvious that by trying to think up more and more ideas, we healthily exercise our imaginative muscles and thus develop our creativeness?

Chapter 23

JOB HUNTING calls for strenuous

idea-hunting

A FAMOUS EMPLOYER URGED that this book include a chapter on how to go about getting a job.

"In my experience," he said, "not one applicant in 500 uses any imagination in applying for a position. Anyone who suggested ideas of possible use to his prospective employer would stand out and be almost sure to get preference—even though his suggestions were unusable."

That kind of creative thinking may be beyond the energy of some of us; but all of us can at least use our vicarious imagination while job-hunting. Instead of putting ourselves into the employer's shoes, too many of us ask him to put himself into ours. This all-too-common fault was recently deplored by the personnel manager of a large corporation:

"Many young men applying to me for jobs these days open their conversations by asking, 'What is your pension plan?' . . . 'If I am discharged will I receive severance pay?' After a few minutes of that sort of talk I interrupt to ask, 'What quality or talent have you demonstrated that makes you think you could help our company earn more money?' At this query, most applicants 'fold their tents like the Arabs,' and as silently steal away."

For 15 years, Sidney Edlund, former head of Lifesavers,

Incorporated, has made it his hobby to teach people how to go after new jobs. His basic principles are these:

1. Offer a service instead of asking for a position.
2. Appeal to the self-interest of your prospective employer.
3. Be specific as to the job you want, and as to your qualifications.
4. Be different, and still be sincere.

All these principles call for thinking ahead, or thinking creatively, or both. Even in the matter of our personal appearance, we might well look into the mirror of imagination before looking for a job. And to be "different"—to lift ourselves above the other applicants—we need to generate ideas before we knock on employers' doors.

2.

We also need imagination to help us set our job-seeking sights. Our first question might well be: "In what vocations would I be most likely to succeed?" Let's jot down all lines that seem at all likely. Having done that, let's use some checklists. Let's run through the classified section of the telephone directory and scan the 200 or so different lines listed there. Then let's go to the library and look over some of the "career" books. Let's talk to some experienced friend and seek his guidance. But let's not make him do our creative thinking for us—let's show him our list of likely lines and ask only for his judgment.

Walter Hoving, of department store fame, estimates that of the 400,000 college graduates looking for jobs each year, only a few think creatively about what to try to do and where to find the right job. "I am constantly staggered," said he, "by this passive waiting for someone else to do the thinking that they should do for themselves."

In choosing our most likely alternatives, we might well project our imaginations into the future by asking ourselves questions such as: "Is the business on the rise?" (Think of those who went to work for traction companies a decade or so ago, and how little chance they have had.) "Will the line be more or less depression-proof?" (If we want to design yachts, the first slump in business may find us with empty drawing-boards.)

And there are many other such thinking-ahead questions. For example, in my early days I was getting along fast in a family-owned manufacturing business. When the proprietor became the father of a son I forced myself to look 25 years ahead, and I foresaw that that baby would eventually head that business. That's how I got out of bed making and into advertising.

The question of questions, however, has to do with our aptitudes. If we are round pegs we should look for round holes. To that end we should do plenty of realistic thinking on our own; and we might well seek vocational guidance.

For many years I watched a boy grow up, confident that eventually he would work in the appliance business which his father owned. After a hitch in the Navy, the young man found himself wondering whether he should become a merchant after all. So he went to a vocational counselor, Dr. Edward S. Jones, psychologist at the University of Buffalo. Aptitude tests indicated that young Alexander Cordes should become a lawyer. He finished his studies with flying colors, was snapped up by a leading law firm, and within one year was asked also to serve as part-time instructor in his law school.

3.

Knowing which vocations we might best explore, we next need to seek openings; and imagination can help a lot in this hunt.

As an example of ingenuity, I like the true story about the young Clevelander who read a "blind" advertisement of just the newspaper job he wanted; but the ad stated only that the opening was in Ohio. He realized that there would be hordes of applicants, and he determined to stand out from the mass. So he secured the names of the managing editors of all the dailies in the state, and wrote letters to each of them. He hit the right man at the right time and landed the job. Two other editors also made him offers.

In writing letters of application we should see ourselves through the eyes of the person addressed. Since nobody wants a slovenly employee, even our spelling is important. A member of the Procter and Gamble personnel department analyzed 500 letters from applicants and found that 82 per cent of them were marred by misspellings.

Instead of individual letters, a job-seeking broadside may be indicated. Robert A. Canyock, about to graduate from Syracuse University, sought a career near his home town. To a list of 170 possible employers, he mailed a folder which was so persuasive that it brought him 32 invitations for interviews. Likewise, Leon Turner, while still a student at Saint Louis University, created a photo-offset brochure which he mailed to 58 companies. A dozen of them replied that they had openings of the kind he was seeking.

A young friend of mine in Missouri was doing well in a municipal job but wanted to get into business as an assistant to a top executive. He prepared a list of industries for which he would like to work, secured the names of the head men and sent them a multigraphed presentation. I have seen this mailing piece; it is an enviable example of creative imagination. Incidentally it led him to exactly the job he wanted.

Another model of creativity was the miniature newspaper put out by William M. Wood, Jr., just before he graduated from the Missouri University School of Journalism. One article told about his scholastic record; another about his Naval service. Another piece related his experience, which included selling want ads for a newspaper; clerking in a grocery store;

laboring in a jewelry factory, in a cannery and on a farm. No wonder he had his pick of 20 offers!

We should be "different" and still be "sincere," as Sidney Edlund advocated. Carl Spier showed me how that principle had been violated by an aspiring ad writer who applied as follows:

"I like fat, buttery words; such as ooze, turpitude, glutinous, toady. I like solemn, angular, creaky words; such as strait-laced, cantankerous, pecunious, valedictory. I like spurious, gold-plated, black-is-white words; such as gentlefolk, mortician, free-lancer, mistress. . . . I like wormy, squirmy, mealy words; such as crawl, blubber, squeal, drip. I like sniggly, chuckling words; such as cowlick, gurgle, bubble and burp. I like words. May I have a few with you?"

Although that got Carl's attention it left him cold.

4.

After a few years in business for myself, I found myself desperately in need of a right-hand man. James H. Rand, Jr., was then starting his little shop which has since grown into Remington Rand, Incorporated. I asked Mr. Rand if he knew of anybody who could team up with me. "Yes," he said, "the other day a salesman came in to see me. I don't remember his name, but I remember that he was from Belmont, New York. You ought to talk to him. He had the cleanest shave I ever saw."

That perfection in appearance led me to track the man down. He turned out to be Clarence L. Davis, and just the associate I sought. He became my partner and a senior vice-president of our company.

That true story illustrates why we should look our best in every way when calling on a prospective employer. Likewise, while at his desk we should deport ourselves punctiliously. Dale G. Casto, who has hired many people, advocates also that applicants should call alone. On this point he says,

"Pull all the strings you can to line up a good interview for yourself but under no circumstances take your father, uncle, or friend with you, even if they want to go. To be shepherded makes you look weak and uncertain of yourself."

Times without number, young people have 'phoned or written to me something like this: "I want to come to see you and ask you about the advertising game." That very question marks the applicant as weak in imaginative energy. In the first place he fails to envision that, when at my office, I am too busy to stop and explain rudiments which anyone could easily learn at the library. Then, too, his query reveals that he has done nothing to appraise his possible value to us, let alone to do any planning for the interview which he requests.

Some employers send representatives to colleges in search of promising young men. An undergraduate friend of mine wanted to work for one of these firms. So he spent four week ends interviewing the company's dealers and competitive dealers. When the representative arrived, he was amazed to find out how much this young man knew about that business. Those two are now at work in the same department.

The higher you aim, the more creative your preparation must be. About a year ago a man who now makes over $25,000 a year decided to go after a better job. He picked the company he wanted to join. He subscribed to all the trade papers in that line of business, and bought all the books that bore on that company's problems. On Saturdays he called on its dealers. After four months of such preparation, he wrote a short note to the head of the company, enclosed an idea for overcoming dealer indifference, and asked for an interview. His plan was turned down; but the officials were so impressed with his grasp of their problems that they offered him the post he had sought.

5.

As part of our preparation for interviews, we should line up the right references. For example, our minister can well attest to our character, but the prospective employer may discount his appraisal of our abilities. On the other hand, the hirer will usually give weight to the words of other executives.

If we go at it creatively enough we can probably sleuth out some mutual friends. If the employer looks over our references and sees the name of an intimate, he will react favorably; because he knows that he can telephone that person and be sure of an honest answer.

Experience, however, carries far more weight than references. If we were to go all out in creative preparation we would see to it that we trained ourselves in advance to make an employer eager for our services.

The late Stanley P. Irvin always wanted to become a journalist. As a farm lad in Illinois, he foresaw that ultimately when seeking a job he would be asked what his experience had been. While attending high school he had to go by train each day from his little village to the county seat where a weekly newspaper was published. He persuaded the editor to let him act as correspondent to cover the other side of the county. Thus during his high school years Stan learned firsthand how to nose out news and how to write it interestingly. Eventually he went to Chicago and landed on the paper of his choice.

6.

A job-seeking interview is a selling interview; and as such it calls for the same type of creative thinking in advance as was described in the last chapter.

In planning our strategy we should ask ourselves all kinds of questions, including plenty of "What-ifs?" For the better we foresee contingencies, the better we can meet them. Thus prepared we can more readily answer questions which otherwise might cause us to say the wrong things, or make us seem slow-minded.

If the employer says, "You need more experience," about the worst remark a job-seeker can make is: "Well, how can I get it if somebody doesn't hire me?" It would be far better to say, "I'm serious about working for you some day. What kind of experience would fit me best for your business?" If the job-seeker then follows his advice, he can go back to him from time to time, report progress, and make progress with him.

Above all, let's go idea-hunting in advance of an interview and think up extras we can offer. Lawrence Terzian in *How to Get the Job You Want* strongly urges this: "Be prepared to show the employer exactly how he can benefit from your services beyond the arbitrary requirements he may have set up, and you will present services he will want to buy. It will be, to him, like making a purchase of a new car. Most cars run, but some, or perhaps one alone, may have added qualities—the 'extras' you want."

7.

So much for the oral phases of our interview. The visual part of our presentation can be just as vital. The United States Navy has proved that people absorb up to 35 per cent more when an appeal is made to the eyes as well as to the ears, and that they retain what they thus learn 55 per cent longer.

Let's not expect the employer to memorize our face and our life story. He sees so many applicants that he will soon forget us unless we leave him something tangible to remember us by. Even so little as a snapshot and a neatly typed summary of our biography will be helpful—and especially so if and when he later discusses us with his associates.

Our visual presentation should be as graphic as possible. A Harvard Business School graduate, after 14 years of successful experience, was applying for a still bigger job. He realized that the conventional summary would make too little a dent. So he drew a pictorial chart which visualized his long experience. This not only intensified the employer's attention, but made him covet the applicant's creative power.

A portfolio complete with samples of work can be a most effective form of presentation. For one thing, this convinces the prospective employer that we are both ingenious and industrious.

A portfolio scores even better when tailor-made to fit the prospect. For example, just after World War II we were taking back 160 of our own people from the armed services and were therefore seeking no new employees. At that very time a young man came to see me and I hired him on the spot. Why? Because he had completed so many missions over Germany and had been decorated so much? No. It was because he had taken three months to study our business and its needs, had thought up just how he could be of most use to us, and had prepared a portfolio especially for that one interview with us—a job of work which proved to me that he was highly creative and in no way allergic to effort.

8.

In planning an interview, we might well think up how to keep the door open should we fail on that first call. Backtracking is almost always necessary in making an important sale; and job-seeking calls for the same kind of selling.

The planning of our follow-up campaign entails still more creative thinking. Points that came out during our first interview can serve as guides, and can indicate pertinent data which we might well gather for further presentation.

The ideal follow-up is a crop of new ideas. When we go back to the employer with more suggestions for the good of his business, we will probably find him eager for our creative thinking, and may find him desirous of our services.

A successful friend of mine, in search of his first job, applied at Macy's. He was flatly told that there were too many applicants ahead of him. Beaten but unbowed, he walked through the store; then he telephoned the personnel director.

"I want a job," he said, "and I've just spent several hours in the store looking for places where I could help. I have listed 10 spots where I think I could be useful right this minute. May I come up and tell you where they are?" Well, you guessed it; he got the interview, and was soon a Macy trainee.

*　　*　　*

George R. Keith was a lawyer who retired at 40. As a creative hobby he conducted a system of finding openings for unemployed people at no expense to them. Over a span of 30 years he contrived ways to help over 80,000 job-seekers. By developing ingenious methods of smoking out opportunities, he was able to find more jobs than people to fill them—even during depressions. He thus proved in a big way that those who use enough creative imagination can usually secure the kind of employment they seek, in slumps as well as in booms.

Chapter 24

HEALTH – how to gird it

with imagination

"MOST OF THE TIME we think we're sick, it's all in the mind," wrote Thomas Wolfe. This may not be 100 per cent so; but substantially it's the truth.

Much depends on whether we use or misuse our imaginations. Creative thinking can help keep us healthy. And maladjustments caused by unwholesome imaginings can often be set right again through creative use of our minds.

Dr. George Crile, the famous surgeon, held that 75 per cent of all sickness is due to tension. Tension is often caused by frustration. Frustration is often caused by failure to overcome our problems. When we master our problems through creative thinking we help defeat frustration and thereby help defeat tension.

Since body and mind are interdependent, it follows that whatever we do to improve our mental health should help our physical health. Thus almost every malady—whether mental or physical or both—presents a creative challenge; and the right use of imagination can be of therapeutic value in nearly every case.

2.

When I visit the workshops of Goodwill Industries, I am torn by two emotions, a feeling of uplift and a sense of shame

—shame that so few of us who visit there can measure up to the self-mastery of those disabled people. I marvel at the brightness of their spirit, just as I have often marveled at how many cripples, like Steinmetz, have become creative titans.

Not long ago I sat and talked with two young women, both of them cruelly crippled. Both of them made their way around New York by themselves, even though, in a normal sense, they were unable to walk. Both of them turned out creative work of high quality and in great quantity. One of them was Betsey Barton, author of books and magazine articles; and the other was Peggy Weiss, editor of a magazine.

Neither one of these young women had shown more than average talent in her childhood. Each had acquired creative ability through an effort to *be* creative as an offset to her fate. According to what they both told me, this strenuous exercise of their imaginations had enabled them to keep both their minds and their bodies in better health than they could otherwise possibly be.

Many a time I have seen H. Katherine Smith walking the avenue, alone except for her Seeing-Eye dog. Although she cannot see, her mind continually visualizes people to write about. She turns out many a feature article, and most of these result from her personal visits to famous persons. Some years ago she and her dog went to France to interview General Eisenhower. Miss Smith will attest that her creativity has helped her mental health.

If and when we are invalided by age, we will be lucky if our imaginations are still aglow. Dr. Albert G. Butzer told me about a call he made on an old woman who had been confined to her room for many years. On her walls she had pasted colored pictures of God's great out-of-doors. In the course of the conversation she said to Dr. Butzer, "Yesterday I was just about at my wits' end. Then I looked at those pictures of Arizona and the Grand Canyon. I imagined I was traveling through that country and soon found myself calm, quiet, and cheerful again."

Many invalids and cripples are living proof of what we can do with our minds—how by continually striving to be more creative we can make ourselves more and more creative —and how by doing this, we can actually help our health.

3.

Although cripples thrive on creative effort, some of the Tarzans in creative crafts claim that "ulcers are the wound stripes" of their professions. As one who spent over 35 years in the hectic pursuit of advertising, I hold no brief for that theory. I agree with Robley Feland—one of the most creative of our craft—who, after 40 years of success as a copy-writer, rendered this verdict: "The occupational disease of advertising men is not ulcers but self-pity."

The prevalence of the ulcer myth is appalling. For example, Robert C. Ruark wrote about a young man who had just been elected to a vice-presidency in his advertising agency and Ruark remarked: "His firm decided that a youngster who was spending several million dollars a year for clients might just as well have a title to go with his ulcers."

In most cases it is not the creative effort which causes nervous indigestion, but the pressure. Some of this is inevitable. Radio and television, for example, are naturally fraught with nerve-racking crises, as I know from personal experience.

In my early days I was in charge of a network show for General Electric emanating from Niagara Falls. We had Graham McNamee on the Rainbow Bridge announcing from a booth we had constructed there. We had one brass band on the American side and another in Canada. Under the Falls we had Phillips Carlin ready to let the listeners hear the roar of Niagara.

Right in the middle of the broadcast, McNamee's smooth script was suddenly deranged by an intruder, the notorious Red Hill. He had outwitted the police guard, had climbed into the booth on the bridge, and had shouted into the microphone: "Tell them about *me*, Graham, tell them about *me!* Tell them about my going over the Falls in a barrel. Tell them about the bodies I've pulled out of the Whirlpool. Tell them about *me.*"

On that hot summer night I started shivering and could not stop. I had to spend the next few days in bed to heal my nerves.

An avoidable drain to our health is pressure caused by our trying to do too much too fast. This usually results from failure to plan ahead and to allow for enough hours. If we apply enough imagination to the sound conduct of our lives we can be far healthier hammering out ideas than driving taxicabs.

Many "creative" ulcers are caused not by working too hard, but by playing too hard. Some advertising craftsmen have been tempted to entertain too much—sometimes for self-entertainment. This abuse, however, is on the wane. For one thing, the good-fellow-well-met technique no longer works with worthwhile clients.

The advertisers themselves are taking an ever stronger stand against entertainment. One morning the head of a large company walked into our office and offered us his million-dollar account, on just one condition: that none of his people would ever be entertained by any of our people and vice versa.

According to Dr. Sidney A. Portis, an authority on gastroenterology, four out of five peptic ulcer cases are caused by emotional disturbances, and not by mental exertion. One emotional disturbance which creative people could avoid is living beyond their means. When they fall into this trap it is usually because they fail to exercise their imaginations in regard to their personal living. By using the same headwork on their private affairs as they use on their jobs, they could probably avoid the ulcerating effect of failing to make ends meet.

For many years I worked with William H. Johns. No advertising man ever put in more creative exertion over the years than he; and yet at the age of 70 I saw him eating pork chops and fried potatoes and feeling bully all the time. The same holds true of the most creative men in other lines. For example, my friend Samuel Hopkins Adams was still hustling around and working full-tilt at the age of 80.

No, it is not creative effort that causes ulcers or any other illness. It is more likely to be lack of creative thinking—failure to apply our imaginations to the problem of how to work hard and yet keep well.

4.

Occupational therapy was well known to ancient Greece. Isn't it strange that our nation went without it until the first World War? Its success since then has piled up proof that effort—especially *creative* effort—can be helpful to health.

Glenn W. Leighbody has personally watched thousands of crippled and disabled people in their struggle toward self-rehabilitation; here's what he concludes: "For the physically handicapped person, work is so important that, without it, other remedial efforts often fail. Exertion usually does much to restore physical and mental health. And the more creative the work, the more therapeutic it is."

Occupational therapy can work wonders even in diseases, according to Dr. L. Maxwell Lockie: "It has been our experience with many patients who are suffering with arthritis that some type of work is essential to convalescence. Also, those people who have residual deformities are much happier if they can do some kind of creative work."

Minor mental ills are often spasms of emotion which cause the mind to grab hold of something unwholesome. "In such cases," said Winston Churchill, "one can insinuate something else into its convulsive grasp. And if this something else is rightly chosen—if it is really attended by the illumination of another field of interest—gradually, and often quite swiftly, the old undue grip relaxes and the process of recuperation and repair begins."

Harry Overstreet echoed the same truth: "He that loses himself in a piece of work that is worth doing finds the kind of life that is wholesomely human." All of us who read *The Mature Mind* will recognize that this statement of Overstreet's referred to work of a creative nature.

It is cheering that of late there has been a trend toward more and more creativity in occupational therapy. A mentally sick person may well be started on straightening crooked nails to induce in him a sense of achievement, no matter how trivial. But as that patient improves, the projects which are mentally more difficult will do more good. Creative feats of any kind will generate the mental glows that mean so much to health.

5.

With all of psychiatry's merits it is the most criticized of all professions. One reason may be that we expect too much. Psychiatry is still a young science, and in the strictest sense it is more of an art than a science. For one thing it must deal with the variables of the human mind, and often with the most elusive phase of our mental make-up, imagination. For the usual psychiatric case stems from imagination gone haywire.

Dr. Theodor Reik, himself a personal friend and disciple of Freud, gives hope in his book, *Listening with the Third Ear,* that psychiatry will outgrow most of its failings. A shortcoming which he scathingly criticizes is his profession's yen for pseudo-scientific mumbo-jumbo, which he calls "psychoanalese." One irritating term in the Freudian lexicon is "Oedipus complex";—defined as "a son's desire to murder his father in order to marry his mother."

Dr. Andrew Salter, in attacking the theory that sex underlies everything, cites this ludicrous example: "Mrs. Smith enjoyed a tap-dancing course at nine years of age, not because she liked to show off, but because she was sexually frustrated. Now Mrs. Smith likes to watch television because it reminds her of the time she peeked through a transom."

A more serious criticism was voiced by Dr. Carney Landis of Columbia University. When asked by the Rockefeller Foundation to undergo a full psychoanalysis and analyze its worth, he quizzed the doctor as to the effect of his technique on a completely normal person. The analyst admitted that it might possibly cause neurosis in such a case. A prominent psychiatrist named Frederic Wertham went even further: "I have reluctantly come to the conclusion that eight out of ten orthodox psychoanalyses are more harmful than helpful."

Psychoanalysis calls for digging up the past, whereas it often may be better to forget than to recall. Immanuel Kant had a servant named Lumpke who was a source of mental disturbance to him. Finally he discharged the man, and put on his desk a sign which read, "Remember to forget Lumpke."

Dr. Alan Gregg of the Rockefeller Foundation criticized "the obsessive search for causes" and urges psychiatrists "to find the meaning of the symptom rather than to find the causes." Thus he put his finger on the profession's need for more reliance on creative imagination and less on analysis.

6.

A paradox of psychoanalysis is that most mental patients are abnormally subjective, and yet psychoanalysis may tend to intensify their subjectivity.

That potential fault has been recognized by a group of psychiatrists in Chicago. They are implementing their therapy with efforts to make their patients more extrovert— to have them change their conduct in their relationships with people to the end that they will act more objectively, and in so doing help root out their introversion.

Another positive measure which is gaining ground in psychiatry is religion. Under the leadership of Dr. Karl A. Menninger, more and more doctors are prescribing this therapy. "Psychiatrists would be blind to ignore the good that spiritual devotion can do," proclaims Dr. Menninger. And in one of his books, *The Way to Security*, Dr. Henry Link reported: "In my work of psychological counseling I have sent hundreds of deluded people to the pastor or to some church as the best solution for their problems."

In England an outstanding psychiatrist, Dr. J. A. Hatfield, recently said this: "Speaking as a student of psychotherapy, who as such has no concern with theology, I am convinced that the Christian religion is one of the most valuable and potent influences for producing that harmony and peace of mind and that confidence of soul which is needed to bring health and power to a large proportion of nervous patients."

The gerontologists who specialize in mental troubles of older people are setting an example for other psychiatrists in that they are guiding their patients to adopt positive measures—to do things—to take on creative activities which will help prevent *mis*use of imagination, and will provide a sense of well-being.

7.

A danger inherent in psychiatry is its tendency to make us lean too much. Although patients should have confidence in their mentors, when the mentally sick put themselves like putty into the hands of others they may thereby aggravate their ills.

Branch Rickey once told me about a pitcher whom he took to a psychiatrist. As a result of the interview the young man found out so many things wrong about his past and about his attitudes that he was able to build up for himself a tasty group of additional alibis. He got plenty of explanation as to why he was the way he was, but no help as to how to make himself the man he should be.

Most athletic coaches would prescribe for that young man a swift kick in the pants. His early success had softened him. He had learned to lean on his coaches; and now he could lean on the psychiatrist and the things the psychiatrist told him. He never did make the grade again as a big-leaguer.

When psychiatrists recommend religion, this implies that we should lean on God; but leaning on God always carries with it an obligation to do something for oneself. Take prayer, for example. "Believers admit no limits to what the power of prayer can do," said Fulton Oursler, "and even skeptics who study the results with an open mind become impressed with the potency of faith. But a man has to meet his Maker half-way; prayer is not a one-way street."

More and more psychiatrists are in agreement with Carlyle's statement: "Work is the grand cure for all the maladies and miseries that ever beset mankind." As the profession gives more weight to the therapy of self-driven effort, it will give ever greater weight to creative effort. Most of all, it will try "to evoke a patient's unused or undiscovered potentialities," as advocated by Dr. Alan Gregg of the Rockefeller Foundation.

8.

Whether our ills be physical or mental, we should recognize them as creative problems and act accordingly. Our suggestions can often help a doctor in his diagnosis and even in his treatment.

Causes of illness can baffle the ablest physician unless we think creatively with him. A physical problem may trace back to a mental problem and a mental problem may trace back to almost anything, including a vocational problem. Dr. William J. Reilly tells about a young newspaperman whose health went bad. He loved to write, but he hated his work. His doctor and he together unearthed the reason—he couldn't stand the competitive pace of reporting. By turning to teaching, and writing books on the side, he regained his health.

Johnson O'Connor tells about a nervous wreck who was engaged in a scientific pursuit which called for the utmost accuracy. Aptitude tests rated him strong in creative imagination and in objectivity. He became a salesman and found his new calling so congenial that his nerves soon healed themselves.

A young man I knew developed boils. The family physician blamed allergies. The dermatologist suspected wool and ruled out all woolen clothing. But the boils raged on; until finally he went to a doctor wise enough to ask: "Have *you* any idea what's causing these boils of yours?" The young man then disclosed a secret worry which was based on wrong imagining. The doctor set him straight, the patient stopped worrying, the boils disappeared. If that young man had thought creatively in the first place, he could have escaped that ordeal.

The possible measures of therapy are so endless that only through the use of creative imagination can a medical mind hit upon a cure. The answer may be as simple as exercise. Dr. Leslie B. Hohman of Johns Hopkins reported the case of an Arizona woman who lost 20 pounds in a short period, developed insomnia, was treated for incipient tuberculosis, and was suspected in turn of heart disease and even cancer. Her outstanding symptom was her emotional disturbance. According to Dr. Hohman the main prescription which brought her back to health was horseback riding.

＊　　＊　　＊

The one therapy which we laymen might well suggest to our doctors and to ourselves is that of *creative* exercise. In most cases we can help mend our minds and bodies by energetically using our imaginations in constructive ways and in line with realities. Thus we can help keep ourselves happier; and happiness is always an aid to health. Moreover, by thus exercising our imaginations we can do much to step up our creative power.

Chapter 25

HAPPINESS can be buttressed

by imagination

ALTHOUGH HEALTH MAY be "the groundwork of all happiness," as Leigh Hunt has said, the most rugged of us can be unhappy. Frequently the cause is a faulty perspective; in such cases the cure can often be the energetic use of imagination—of the right kind and in the right way.

The problem of keeping cheerful cuts through all economic lines. Dr. Norman Vincent Peale, who has dealt with both the rich and the ragged, believes that contentment is less likely to be the property of the wealthy than of those in modest circumstances. "In my interview work," he reported, "I find more personality disorganization among the favored class than among the common run of folk." And Dr. Henry van Dyke expressed a similar belief: "Happiness is inward, and not outward; and so it does not depend on what we have, but on what we are."

What we are depends on what we do—whether, for example, we let imagination work against us or make it work for us. In the words of Margaret Broadley: "A directed and usefully employed creative imagination offers a chance for a deeply satisfying life through the release of creative forces. But imagination must be guided. Left to itself, it can play hob with its possessor."

If we look at it right, even pain can have its good points.

245

Sometimes it is a helpful warning of a malady which we might otherwise ignore until too late. When pain is of a known cause, we can minimize its hurt—as when faced with oral surgery we can make ourselves think, "What if this were my eye instead of my tooth?" And almost always we can project our imagination to the time when our pain will have passed.

Although some realists may look down upon such rationalizing, the fact is that we still would be in the dark ages were it not for wishful thinking. Without it most of the achievements of mankind would never have been started.

And in our personal lives, the seeing-is-believing attitude can harm us. Unless we let imagination *help* us to see, we improverish our souls—we become victims of the anemia described by Samuel Hoffenstein:

Little by little we subtract faith and fallacy from fact,
The illusory from the true, and starve upon the residue.

2.

Even the strongest spirits are prone to sag. Karl Menninger described President Lincoln's depressions as so deep that, during one period, "it was necessary to watch him every hour of the day and night. At one time it was considered advisable to remove all knives, scissors, and other instruments with which he might have taken his life."

There were real reasons for Lincoln's melancholy. On the other hand, the blues that beset most of us are seldom due to crushing causes. These spells can often be prevented, or relieved by the right use of creative imagination.

In general, our normal depressions are of two types—the fairly chronic and the kind that's here today and gone tomorrow. Dr. Donald A. Laird's theory is that blues are due to emotional cycles. A more understandable principle is that of action and reaction. Elation often brings depression in its train. Madame Chiang Kai-shek pointed this out when she told how, after her religion had lifted her to new heights, her spirits then sank. "I was plunged into dark despair," she said. "A terrible depression settled on me."

Although Monday blues come in weekly cycles they are due to physical habits rather than to emotional causes, according to George Ross Wells: "On Sunday, most persons eat, work, and sleep according to an entirely different program than the usual one. The organism is thereby thrown slightly out of gear, and the mild disorder is partly manifested in the unpleasant conviction on the next day that nothing is worth while."

When spirits sag from such causes they usually bounce back. The more chronic cases, however, need our creative help. These are often due to a physical or mental disorder. Colitis, for example, has caused many a long siege of despondency. Among the mental causes, emotional disturbances and dire forebodings predominate. Self-pity is often a complication if not a contributory cause.

At my request a professor friend of mine asked members of his class to write what they did to beat the blues. One frank young man handed in this report over his signature: "When I feel depressed I use one of these methods to revive myself: (1) I cut class and go to a show in the middle of an afternoon; or (2) I go out and buy myself a hat I don't need, or a dozen neckties; or (3) I get stinking drunk."

Dale Carnegie's suggestion for killing gloom is that we sit down and imagine we have lost everything we hold precious—family, house, job and health. Thus we generate the very bluest of thoughts. Then we pound home to ourselves, "But that's not so! I haven't lost any of them! I can be happy because I still have them!"

Instead of just musing, we might even write up our case. The chances are it won't look so gruesome on paper—it may even look ridiculous enough to make us laugh at ourselves. And the very fact of that writing effort may produce an emotional release—may open the gate for some creative thinking on our own.

When our depression stems from a mistake we have made, we might well call to mind that everybody errs. We might even laugh off our boners as Fiorello LaGuardia did. "When I make a mistake it's a big one," he once said by way of self-cheer.

We can sometimes overcome gloom by changing shoes— such as listening to someone else's troubles. Or we might think up places to go—to a show, to a concert, to the home of a friend, or to church. "Lots of people take their troubles to church and leave them there."

Even in his youth Abraham Lincoln was subject to depression. In such a state, he called on his friends the Speeds, and Mrs. Speed gave him a Bible which she recommended as a remedy for despondency. Later he wrote to her daughter: "Tell your mother I doubt not that it is really as she says, the best cure for the blues."

Or we might take on some physical exercise and, best of all, some creative exercise—as I proved to myself one morning when an untoward incident sent my spirits into a tailspin. It was important that I get myself back into the right mood for a conference that afternoon at which I was due to preside. So I hit upon the plan of going to lunch alone and tackling a crazy creative project.

A few weeks before, Grantland Rice and I had been talking about a silly idea of mine for a piece of verse. So at the Hotel Statler that noon, on the back of the menu, I scribbled seven quatrains on that theme. The people at nearby tables probably wondered what asylum I was from. But I had fun; and I returned to the office in good spirit.

Just keeping busy can do a lot either to prevent or cure depressions. "I never knu a man trubbled with melankolly, who had plenty to dew, and did it." Those were the words which Henry Wheeler Shaw put into the mouth of Josh Billings nearly a century ago. Hobbies, as well as work, can be bulwarks against blues. And the more creative they are the better they make us feel.

Then, too, when we know we are in for something that can't be avoided it may help if we steer our imagination into it head-on. For instance, during my third fevered day of flu, I said to my wife: "If this runs true to form I will be all over it by next Monday and then I'll be depressed for two days." A week later I was back at work but almost as low as a dachshund. I would have been even more dispirited had I not projected my imagination—had I not conditioned myself against that mental slump.

3.

A popular song proclaims: "You may be as brave as you make believe you are." This, of course, is an exaggeration; but it is quite true that, just as unbridled imagination may cause fear, creative imagination can generate courage.

According to Erich Fromm, "Rational anxiety due to the awareness of realistic dangers operates in the service of self-preservation; it is an indispensable and healthy part of our psychic organization. The absence of fear is a sign of either lack of imagination and intelligence, or a lack in one's will to live."

There are big fears and little fears, justifiable fears and unfounded fears. If the dread is big and real, it can best be met with faith—basic faith, such as the fact that day has never yet failed to dawn. "Courage is fear that has said its prayers."

Saint Paul was famed for his triumphs over fear. His courage was contagious. When shipwrecked, he gave his crew a fight talk: "But now I exhort you to be of good cheer." That such a ringing call could exert a powerful influence is easy to understand. Although Saint Paul was small of stature, he stood on the deck of that storm-tossed ship like a colossus. His brand of faith generates the kind of courage which can conquer panic.

Another way we can use creative imagination to offset fear is to think up all possible alternatives. A classic example of this technique was demonstrated in Franz Werfel's play, *Jacobowsky and the Colonel.* Their Polish regiment had just lost 3000 of its men trying to keep the Germans out of Paris. Jacobowsky, seeing an old lady about to faint from fright, grips her arm and says to her:

"Courage, Madame. My poor mother, wise woman that she was, always used to say that no matter what happens in life there are always two possibilities. It is true. For example, right now it is a dark moment and yet even now there are two possibilities. The Germans—either they'll come to Paris, or they'll jump to England. If they don't come to Paris, that's good. But if they should come to Paris, again there are two possibilities. Either we succeed in escaping, or we don't succeed. If we succeed, that's good, but if we don't there are always two possibilities. The Germans, either they'll put us in a good concentration camp or in a bad concentration camp. If in a good concentration camp, that's good, but if they put us in a bad concentration camp, there are still two . . ."

In that situation the ground for fear was real. Most anxiety, however, is mainly of our own imagining. For example, fear of the unknown is the oldest obsession of mankind. And we even manufacture fear out of things we know about—like the little girl who, when summoned by her mother, exclaimed: "Oh, Mama, you disturbed me! I was just getting frightened about our new car and now I can't remember why."

One foolish fear is that which grips us when we lie awake against our will. We magnify insomnia as a disease which will destroy us. Thus we misuse our imagination—whereas, by thinking creatively, we could combat this fear, and might even induce sleep.

Maxine Davis wrote: "The old-fashioned trick of counting sheep has been replaced by a new one, invented by psychologists: 'free association.' The insomniac is told to think of one object and then leap rapidly to the next thing it suggests. For example, if the word 'nuts' occurs to him, he may say 'beech-nuts.' That reminds him of 'tree,' which reminds him of 'shade,' and so on. He should never pause to consider any of these subjects. In a short time, he probably will fall asleep." Thus, by putting into gear the automatic part of imagination, we can drive ourselves to slumberland.

4.

The wise men of yesterday tried to warn us against worry. Said Thomas Jefferson, "Tranquillity of mind depends much upon ourselves and greatly on due reflection. How much pain have cost us the evils which have never happened!" A century later, another president, James A. Garfield, observed: "I have had many troubles in my life, but the worst of them never came."

One way to allay worry is to attack it creatively—to run one's mind into channels where sailing is smoother. For instance, when our anxiety is caused by a plethora of bad news, we can make our minds reach out for good tidings. And there is plenty of such, as was proved in the *Saturday Review of Literature* by Joseph M. Grant, who had assembled scores of beneficent items which had been hidden in the newspapers of the recent past. One of these was the fact that the nation is now the healthiest in its history. Another was that in the last elections, more citizens went to the polls than ever before in a non-presidenial election. And so it went, page after page.

We can push anxiety out of our minds by pushing something creative into them. Winston Churchill was never more worried than during the second half of 1915. As First Lord of the Admiralty he had plenty to keep his mind off the horrible things that were happening. But, having gone from that exciting post, he had too much time to brood. "I had long hours of utterly unwonted leisure in which to contemplate the frightful unfolding of the war. At a moment when every fiber of my being was inflamed to action, I was forced to remain a spectator of the tragedy, placed cruelly in a front seat. And then it was that the Muse of Painting came to my rescue."

But even better than such hobbies are the more strenuous imaginative exercises—such as energetically tackling causes of our worry and thinking our way through to serenity.

5.

In his *Road to a Richer Life*, Walter Pitkin wrote: "Boredom is an insidious disease. It plagues millions, kills some, drives others mad, and is overcome only by strong minds."

The reason why so many shut-ins seem so far from forlorn was explained by Washington Irving: "It is the divine attribute of the imagination that it is irrepressible, unconfinable; that when the real world is shut out, it can create a world for itself, and with necromantic power can conjure up glorious shapes and forms, and brilliant visions to make solitude populous, and irradiate the gloom of a dungeon."

Far too many cases of loneliness are due to idleness—to "being fed up" with things. "A wise man is never less alone than when he is alone," wrote Swift two centuries ago. And there is nothing wiser than to keep creatively busy. When we do this we can at least enjoy the companionship of our minds.

"A mind is never a better companion than when it is busy with a new idea," wrote H. A. Overstreet. "We are happily engaged when we try to turn an old situation we do not quite like, into a new one that we can like better. There is some place to go with a mind like that, just as surely as there is some place to go with a good friend."

A Britisher recently came up with these three questions as tests of an educated man: "Can you entertain a new idea?"

. . . "Can you entertain another person?" . . . "Can you entertain yourself?"

When we try to entertain ourselves through the usual forms of escape, we invite further boredom. A far better way is to exercise our creativity as Henry J. Taylor has done. As a result of his inventive effort, he acquired a fortune while still young. If he had idled from then on he probably would have become bored to death. Instead, he took on new forms of creative effort, and by practice became an internationally known writer. In a recent network broadcast he urged:

"Be workers, for the daily work is the daily bread. But also be dreamers, seers of visions, makers of plans, believers in greater possibilities—more and better things for more people. Cling to your imagination—to the power of planning and hoping and believing, the power to defeat dullness and stagnation."

6.

Age too often brings in its wake both loneliness and boredom. But, at sunset, we can make our lives far more livable if we accept the philosophy of Logan Pearsall Smith: "Let Youth be the time for adventures of the body, and make Age the time for triumphs of the mind."

Unless we keep imagination alive, we might better die than retire. The loneliest man I know is a banker who quit work after 50 years of glorifying cold figures and discounting ideas. The only use he makes of his imagination is to dream up ailments for himself. He thinks he thinks; but his mind dwells on the past. And that's not thinking—that's just letting one's memory run around in a squirrel cage.

How old is old? Some people are old at 30, others are youthful at 80. A lifelong friend of mine who had risen to the top of his field wrote me on a recent birthday: "How do you like being 60? Neither do I." This shocked me, because it found me feeling quite happy. Why? Partly because I was trying harder than ever before to be more creative and in more different ways.

If we used our imaginations well enough we would foresee the day when our labors would end and boredom might set in; and early in life we would devise ways to brighten our journey down the other side of the hill. Such a program would most certainly call for the development of our creativeness by taking on activities which could help keep our minds awake throughout life.

Dr. Walter C. McKain, Jr., Associate Professor of Rural Sociology at the University of Connecticut, studied many an old couple. His conclusion was that the happiest among them were those who, while young, developed a variety of interests not connected with their work. Dr. McKain strongly advises that we lay foundations for our retirement during our early years. "If a person knows he must retire some day," Dr. McKain says, "he should take an inventory of his interests and hobbies and determine whether or not they will be sufficient to keep him happy."

Jean Rindlaub, who was chosen as "The Advertising Woman of 1951," told a group of grown-up girls: "I've seen many women of over 40 who have lost their grip, lost their hope, lost their capacity to have fun and to laugh at themselves. And I've seen many others who are still growing gloriously in their middle age. The time to make the decision as to which kind of woman to be is not when your hair has begun to gray, but right now when you're still young."

Stephen Cole gave a case-history of a woman who, at 60, was so bored that she was actually sick. In his conclusion he says that if she had started early enough "in arts and hobbies and other forms of creation she would have been different. Painting would have saved her. So might writing poetry. If she had thrown her energies into any of these things she would have been an ever-growing woman. Instead she died, but was not buried, before she was 40."

There can be no doubt that Voltaire spoke the truth in saying: "Creative effort keeps boredom at bay." And this applies to the young as well as the old.

7.

A helpful use of the imagination in regard to age is to acquire proper perspective. William Lyon Phelps stressed this when he wrote:

"As we advance in years we really grow happier, if we live intelligently. To live abundantly is like climbing a mountain or a tower. To say that youth is happier than maturity is like saying that the view from the bottom of the tower is better than the view from the top. As we ascend, the range of our views widens immensely; the horizon is pushed farther away. Finally, as we reach the summit, it is as if we had the world at our feet."

Many who could retire prefer to take on new worlds for their creative minds to conquer. Clarence Birdseye is one of them. He recently reported: "In my own case, life has been an exciting adventure since my earliest remembrance, and today, at 64, I am having just as much fun as I ever did. I am never bored, because I am always prying into something or other which fascinates me."

Others follow the plan facetiously recommended by William Feather: "What I want is the privilege of retiring until I feel like working again. It might not take long, boss." One couple who did just that were the Jarvises, of Hamilton, Ontario. Ernest Jarvis had made a success in the chemical field, and finally became president of a big company in Niagara Falls. His wife served as his secretary. He sold out for a million and retired at 50. "We had nothing to do," Jarvis said later. "We went to 77 ball games the first Summer. We were bored stiff." Finally they went back to work for the company which had bought them out. They have been having the time of their lives ever since.

That the boredom of retirement can be averted by creative thinking has been proved by a group of pensioners who had been turned out to pasture in Wilmington, Delaware. Instead of lying down and chewing their cuds, these oldsters are having a romping good time getting their teeth into the problems of small businesses in need of big-time guidance. The man who thought up this idea is Maurice Du Pont Lee. And it is he who heads this unique organization called "Consulting and Advisory Services, Inc." By creatively attacking problem after problem, these old-timers are keeping their brain-cells alive and their spirits up.

* * *

Those of us who keep on trying to be creative are sure to become more and more creative. Thus we build up our resources for happiness, even to the point where our winters of discontent may never come.

Chapter 26

CHARACTER can grow with

creative development

FINALLY, LET'S CONSIDER a few positive ways in which we can use imagination not only to build cheer but to build character. There are two kinds of giving which can help us toward both goals: (1) Thanksgiving; (2) Forgiving.

At a Thanksgiving assembly, our Sunday School Superintendent asked the pupils to stand up and tell why they were grateful. "I am thankful for my mother and daddy," was the typical answer of the older children. The Superintendent tried to ignore the curly-hair five-year-old who kept her hand held high. Finally he felt forced to ask her, "Well, little girl, what have you to be thankful for?" To which my daughter replied: "I'm thankful for baked bananas."

To me that story is more significant than amusing. I have seen that little girl grow into a mother. She still practices gratitude, and she agrees that this is one reason why she seems happier than most young parents who have to take care of three little children, two kittens and a cocker spaniel—with no full-time help.

The therapy of giving thanks is based on a sound psychological principle. As Walter Pitkin wrote: "Every shift of attention is a shift of tensions. Every shift of tensions breaks down (more or less) the bad effects of the previous tension—

hence it is good. The most effective way of shifting attention is to shift attitudes."

The "attitude of gratitude" is strongly recommended by Dr. Norman Vincent Peale. In his *Guide to Confident Living* he wrote: "Students of the dynamic power of thought are realizing the tremendous value of the practice of thanksgiving in making people happier." He then goes on to point out that we can test this for ourselves. When we arise in the morning and say things like "What a terrible night I had," we are licked for that day before we start. On the other hand, if our first remarks are by way of gratitude for our blessings we are likely to feel better all day long and to act better toward others.

In his religio-psychiatric clinic at the Marble Collegiate Church, Dr. Peale continually prescribes the technique of thanksgiving. He suggests an average of three prayers a day—one in which the suppliants ask for something, the other two in which they express gratitude. "This is a technique we have seen revolutionize the lives of hundreds of gloomy, discouraged, ineffective people," reports Dr. Peale.

Another way to practice thanksgiving is to list the many blessings we enjoy—such as the fact that we have a hand with which to write, that we live in the United States and not under a totalitarian tyranny. The list will be convincingly long if we think hard enough.

Having read my last book, a stranger wrote me in longhand that he was 36 years old, "married to a fine wife, father of two swell boys, and owner of a successful business." Despite all that, said he, "I remain discontented and seem to have no peace of mind." He asked me for my advice and here's what I wrote him:

"You are a fortunate person. Less than one in 1000 can boast of a business of his own. Then, too, yours is an ideal family. Therefore, the first thing you should do is to count your blessings."

Nearly all of us, if we think creatively, will feel like getting down on our knees whenever we inventory our fortunes. Such thanksgiving makes for the right kind of humility which, in turn, makes for the right kind of character.

2.

To turn the other cheek—this, too, calls for imagination. In my early days I wrote an article for a trade magazine and received a small check in return. The piece appeared under the name of an assistant editor as its author. At first I was mad; but then I figured that he had done me no real damage—that by falling for that temptation he had harmed himself far more than me. Thus, I rose above my anger.

To forgive, we must put ourselves into the shoes of those who wrong us. And we must turn our imagination upon ourselves and realize that if we were they *we* would want to be forgiven.

Many a son leaves home to sow his wild oats and later asks to be taken back. If his parents let their emotions hold sway they may lose him forever. But if they tackle his homecoming as a creative problem, they will realize that the best hope, both for him and for them, is to greet him with a forgiving welcome.

Only through use of our imaginations can we foresee the harm we do by *not* forgiving—foresee the sundered relationships which not even time can mend—foresee the damage we do to our own characters by keeping our grudges stewing.

3.

The gains from giving are great. For one thing we make ourselves more wanted. Another emolument is that we like ourselves better. The importance of such self-esteem has been stressed by psychiatrist Dr. Alexander Reid Martin: "If people had a healthy love of themselves instead of carrying hidden burdens of self-contempt, our psychiatric case-load would be cut in half."

Those who give of themselves grow more attractive. "There is no beautifier like the wish to scatter joy," wrote William Driver. And James M. Barrie likewise held that benefaction makes us radiant: "Those who bring sunshine to the lives of others cannot keep it from themselves."

It takes imagination to realize that we can enrich our lives by giving. When we sense this truth—and *live* it—we attain a trait that helps make our characters shine.

4.

"The hours we pass with happy prospects in view," said Oliver Goldsmith, "are more pleasing than those crowned with fruition." We all know that this is true; yet few of us know that we can multiply such hours through conscious use of imagination. Sometimes, through creative expectancy, we can even look forward to something we want to come true and *make* it come true.

Ofttimes it is unwise to let imagination have too free a rein; but we unduly rob ourselves if we keep our minds from projecting pictures of good things ahead. Ralph Waldo Emerson approved of this pleasure when he said: "I find the gayest castles in the air that were ever piled, far better for comfort and for use than the dungeons that are daily dug and caverned out by grumbling, discontented people."

Bruce Barton once did an editorial about creative expectancy. "It is snowing outside," he wrote. "The sky is leaden; no birds sing. The winter wind howls. And I have been lying on my back, reading a seed catalogue, and laughing to myself at poor old Winter. I know positively that I have him beaten. I have even marked down on my calendar the date in April when I shall celebrate my victory by my annual triumphal march." And then he goes on to tell how, stretched out on his city sofa on that February evening, he revels in the sunshine and other glories of Spring—thanks to the power of his anticipative imagination.

In business, most of those who rise to the heights are carried upward by their creative expectancy. E. M. Statler was such a man. When he built his little inn outside the Pan American Exposition grounds in Buffalo in 1900, he had in view a chain of great hotels. Over 30 years ago he said to me, "There will even be a Statler Hotel some day out on the Pacific Coast." The edifice he erected in Los Angeles 25 years later was probably even then in his imagination.

Mary McLeod Bethune started her Negro college on a dump in Florida with only a little cabin, a few drygoods boxes, and five pupils. When she asked James M. Gamble, of Procter and Gamble, to be a trustee he replied: "What do you want me to be a trustee of?"

"I want you to be the trustee of the thing I have in mind to create." The great Bethune-Cookman College of today is a monument to the creative expectancy which she then expressed.

5.

The right kind of character is marked by a true sense of values. How do we develop this trait? By judgment—by comparing this against that? Yes, but also by imagination. Otherwise, we would give too much weight to the immediate and the obvious. Only by foreseeing the ultimate can we acquire a true perspective.

Hell's fire was formerly a mental picture which helped deter many of us from committing sin. The fact that the devil is no longer looming so vividly in our mind's eye may help explain the rise of crime. When tempted, we may be unable to bring brimstone to our nostrils, but we can at least put ourselves into the shoes of others who have paid too high a price for their transgressions. We can even visualize them in their prison garb.

If we make a list of our good traits and our bad traits, we can readily see how, by the right use of imagination, we can fortify our virtues and cut down on our faults.

We are born selfish. We develop enlightenment by envisioning the blind alleys into which egoism may take us. We are born greedy. We overcome our rapacity by foreseeing how our overreaching may defeat itself.

Most of us are lazy by nature. We overcome indolence largely by visualizing where it will lead us. We develop a sense of responsibility by imagining how we would like it if others shirked their duties, as well as by weighing the consequences to us of our *own* slacking.

We are born intolerant. We develop magnanimity through putting ourselves into the other fellow's shoes, and hoping that he will put himself into ours.

We are born arrogant. We develop humility by seeing ourselves as others see us—and by otherwise developing a sense of values.

Even faith itself is a product of our creative minds. As Henry J. Taylor said: "Our imagination is the key to reverence, the bridge in our daily union with God." Or as Bishop Austin Pardue said, "Through imagination we can lift ourselves above our egos and make Christ more a part of us."

The core of personality is character, and personality, in turn, largely depends on what we do with our minds.

"Not every person may become a personage," wrote William Lyon Phelps, "but every person may become a *personality*." To achieve that goal, however, we must keep our minds awake—we must see to it that our characters mature in the creative ways which Harry Overstreet prescribed.

We will then be doing our best by ourselves, and perhaps may be helping mankind. For as Hughes Mearns wrote, "The development of one's creative self is the open door to a wise and peaceful life, and if widely employed may even be the hope of a tortured world."

*   *   *

Creative imagination—the lamp that lit the world—can light our lives. God grant that likewise it may light our way to world peace.

INDEX